Includes authentic video from the BBC

British 4
News
Update

Timothy Knowles   Minne Tanaka

Mihoko Nakamura   Sayaka Moue

KINSEIDO

Kinseido Publishing Co., Ltd.
3-21 Kanda Jimbo-cho, Chiyoda-ku,
Tokyo 101-0051, Japan

First published 2022 by Kinseido Publishing Co., Ltd.

Text design & Editorial support   C-leps Co., Ltd.

BBCニュース ホームページ：www.bbc.com/news

The British Broadcasting Corporation (BBC) is internationally famous for the quality and impartiality of its news items. BBC reporters also strive to make the news both interesting and as easy to understand as possible. In this book we have chosen 15 items that we think would be of particular interest, and therefore motivating. They are mainly about Britain, as you might expect, and learners will gain an insight into the life and culture of that country. However, many of the issues covered, such as health, education, and the environment, are also important in Japan, so there is the opportunity to discuss and compare the two countries.

There were two issues in particular which dominated the British scene in 2020 and 2021. Firstly, of course, there is the coronavirus pandemic, still a serious problem at the time of this issue going to print. Two of the units examine the effects of the lockdowns on education and careers, and it should also be noted that most of the videos in this issue were made under coronavirus distance limitations. Secondly, at the end of January 2021, Britain officially left the EU. We have been able to include one unit about the initial effects this has had on our trade with Europe, but we do not know yet what the full effects will be. These will certainly be covered in our next issue.

As ever, new items of vocabulary are explained, and the notes (in Japanese) will explain any interesting points of grammar and usage of English. However the most important purpose of this book is that the learners should be able to engage in the subject matter, research, and then discuss together. With this in mind, we have developed discussion questions that would encourage them to relate these new discoveries with what is already familiar to them.

The videos are easily accessible online. This will make it easy for students to study by themselves out of class.

We hope you enjoy the book and the videos.

はじめに

　本書は、実際に放送されたBBC（英国放送協会）のニュースを教材として、ニュースキャスターや街頭インタヴューを受けるnative speakerが自然に話す英語に触れることで、学習者のリスニング力や語彙力といった英語力を伸ばすことを目的としています。同時に、イギリスや世界で起こっている出来事やその背景となる社会や文化についても学べるように工夫されています。

　扱うトピックは、政治、経済、環境などから、昨今世界中で猛威を振るっている新型コロナウイルス関連まで多岐にわたるものとし、できるだけup to dateでありつつも普遍的なものを選びました。学習する皆様の興味関心の幅を広げ、ご希望にお応えすることができれば幸いです。

　前作に引き続き、ユニット内のコラムは、イギリス文化についての興味深い情報を増やして充実を図り、Questionsも最初の **Setting the Scene** に始まり **Follow Up** にいたるまで、各ユニットで取り上げるニュースを順序良く掘り下げて理解が深まるように配慮しました。

　本書を通じて、伝統と革新が共存する多民族国家イギリスが、4つの地域の独自性を保ちつつ、総体としてのイギリスらしさ（"Britishness"）を模索する今の姿を見ていただけると思います。現在のイギリスは、EUからの離脱やスコットランドの独立問題に加え、新型コロナウイルスによる混乱の渦中にあり、日本や世界に与える影響を考慮すると、今後もその動きから目が離せません。

　このテキストを使って学習する皆様が、イギリスや世界の状勢に興味を持ち、さらには、自分から英語ニュースに触れたり、英語で意見を述べたりと、ますます学習の場が広がっていきますことを、執筆者一同願っております。

　最後になりましたが、本書の作成にあたり、BBCニュースを教材として使うことを許可してくださいましたBBC、編集に際してご尽力いただきました金星堂の長島吉成様とシー・レップスの佐伯亜希様に、この場をお借りして心より感謝申し上げます。

テキストの特徴

　普段の生活の中で、ニュースの英語に触れる機会はあまりないかもしれません。本テキストは、初めて英語でニュースを観る場合でも無理なく取り組めるよう、多種多様なアクティビティを用意しています。単語のチェックや内容確認、穴埋め、要約、ディスカッションを通して、段階を踏みながらニュースを理解できるような作りになっているので、達成感を感じることができるでしょう。

Starting Off

1. Setting the Scene

　実際にニュースを観る前に、ニュースで扱われるトピックについて考えるためのセクションです。トピックについての学習を始めるにあたり、身近な問題としてトピックを捉えられるような問題を用意しました。ここで先にニュースに関する情報を整理しておけば、実際にニュースを観る際に理解が容易になります。ニュースで使われている単語や語句、または重要な概念をここで予習しておきましょう。

2. Building Language

　ニュースの中で使われる重要単語を学びます。単に日本語の訳語を覚えるのではなく、英語での定義を通して、また同義語を覚えながら、単語の持つ意味を英語で理解することを目指します。また、これらの単語はディスカッションを行うときにもおそらく頻繁に使うことになる単語ですし、ニュースの核となる単語ですので、発音もしっかりと確認することが重要です。

Watching the News

3. Understanding Check 1

　実際にニュースの中身を詳しく見ていく前に、どんな意見が交わされているのかを確認します。ここで具体的にニュースのイメージをつかむことが大事です。全体像を簡単にでも把握することで、ニュース理解の大きな助けとなります。

4. Understanding Check 2

　ニュースに関する問題を解くことで、どれだけニュースを理解できたか確認することができます。間違えた箇所に関しては、なぜ間違えたのかをしっかりと分析し、内容を正確に把握しましょう。**Filling Gaps** のアクティビティを行ってから **Understanding Check 2** に取り組むのも効果的かもしれません。

5. Filling Gaps

　ニュースの中で重要な意味を持つ単語を聞き取ります。何度も繰り返し聞き、正しい発音を意識します。それと同時に、単語を正しく書き取ることで、耳と手との両方の動きを通して重要単語を習得することを目指します。もし時間に余裕があれば、穴埋めの単語を実際に発音し、耳と手に加え口も使って覚えると効果的です。

Moving On

6. Making a Summary

　この箇所は、これまで観てきたニュースをまとめる部分でもあり、かつ **Follow Up** に至る前の準備の段階でもあります。しっかりと内容を理解しているか、このアクティビティを通して確認しましょう。また、**Building Language** で出てきた単語を再度使っているため、単語の習熟の確認ができるようになっています。

7. Follow Up

　ニュースと関連したトピックをいくつか挙げてあります。ニュースで得た知識、また単語を活かして話し合いを行うためのセクションです。トピックには、その場で話し合えるものと各自調べてから発表し合うもの、両方が含まれています。そのニュースに関してだけでなく、今後似たような話題に接したときにも意見を述べることができるよう、このアクティビティで仕上げを行います。

Background Information

　ニュースでは、必ずしもすべての事柄が説明されているとは限りません。ニュースの核となる事柄で、かつニュースの中ではあまり詳しく説明されていないことに関して、このセクションでは補足しています。ニュースをより深く理解するのにも役立ちますし、**Follow Up**での話し合いの際にも使えるかもしれません。

Behind the Scenes

　ニュースに関連することではありますが、**Background Information** とは異なりここではニュースの核となることではなく、話題が広がる知識、教養が深まる知識を取り上げました。肩の力を抜き、楽しんで読めるような内容になっています。

・ 各ユニットで取り上げたニュース映像はオンラインで視聴することができます。詳しくは巻末を参照ください。
・ テキスト準拠の Audio CD には、各ユニットのニュース音声と、ニュースを学習用に聞き取りやすく吹き替えた音声、Making a Summary を収録しています。

Contents

Map of The United Kingdom

正式名称は **The United Kingdom of Great Britain and Northern Ireland**（グレートブリテン及び北アイルランド連合王国）。**England**（イングランド）、**Wales**（ウェールズ）、**Scotland**（スコットランド）、**Northern Ireland**（北アイルランド）の4国から成る連合国家です（2021年現在）。

North Atlantic Ocean

※（ ）は本テキストでその地名、場所が登場
　するユニットを表します

Greater London

**Highgate
Cemetery**
(Unit 4)

**Hampstead
Heath** (Unit 9)

Tufnell Park
(Unit 11)

Wembley
(Unit 11)

Hackney
(Unit 8)

Piccadilly
(Unit 2)

Soho (Unit 3)

Haveri
(Unit 1)

Kensington

River Thames

Hammersmith
Bridge (Unit 4)

Carnaby Street
(Unit 10)

Crystal Palace
(Unit 1)

Inverness

Scotland

North
Sea

Northern
Ireland

Glasgow

Belfast

Isle of Man

Newcastle
(upon Tyne)

York

Irish Sea

Ireland

Conwy

England

Birmingham

Wales

Cambridge

**Sizewell,
Suffolk**
(Unit 12)

the Chilterns
(Unit 6)

Oxford

Marlow
(Unit 6)

Cardiff
(Unit 14)

Reading
(Unit 3)

**Hinkley Point,
Somerset** (Unit 12)

Portsmouth

Dover

St. Ives

Plymouth

Isle of Wight

Brooklands
(Unit 7)

Unit 1

An Award for an Unsung Hero

新型コロナウイルスのパンデミックという苦境の中、人々のために働いてきたスポーツの
コーチが、ある賞を受賞しました。どのようなものでしょうか。ニュースを見てみましょう。

Starting Off

1 Setting the Scene

▶ What do you think?

1. What is your favourite sport or exercise?
2. Can you remember a person who introduced you to sport, or think of someone who encouraged you?
3. Have you ever thought of doing a triathlon (running, swimming and cycling)? Why do you think so many people like to do it?

2 Building Language

▶ Which word (1-5) best fits which explanation (a-e)?

1. qualify   [   ]   **a.** pass a test or show that you have the skills necessary for a job or position
2. inspire   [   ]   **b.** succeed in reaching a target or goal
3. monetise   [   ]   **c.** encourage or give hope to somebody
4. remotely   [   ]   **d.** make money from an idea
5. achieve   [   ]   **e.** from a distance

3 Understanding Check 1

▶ Read the quotes, then watch the news and match them to the right people.

1. ... whereas my reward isn't money. [　]

2. Audrey thoroughly deserves this award. [　]

3. ... over an audio link, and gives you instructions over headphones. [　]

4. ... one woman from the capital who's worked tirelessly to encourage more people ... [　]

4 Understanding Check 2

▶ Which is the best answer?

1. What did Audrey Livingston do in her forties?
   a. She gave up her job as a coach.
   b. She found an advertising job.
   c. She qualified as a driver.
   d. She started doing triathlons.

2. Why does Audrey prefer being a coach to being in advertising sales?
   a. In advertising, her only reward was money, but as a coach, people tell her how they feel.
   b. She earns more money as a coach than she did in advertising sales.
   c. She gets a bonus at the end of the month, but in advertising she didn't.
   d. She has lost a lot of weight since becoming a coach.

3. Which of the following sentences is correct?
   a. Audrey had never heard of the Unsung Hero Award.
   b. Audrey already knew that she had won the Unsung Hero Award.
   c. Audrey knew about the Unsung Hero Award, but didn't know that she had won.
   d. Audrey was surprised that she hadn't won the Unsung Hero Award.

4. What is the purpose of Soul Swimmers?

_____

5. What was Audrey's brilliant idea, according to the man?

_____

6. Why did the woman from South London think Audrey deserved the award?

_____

BACKGROUND INFORMATION

　「BBCスポーツ・パーソナリティ・オブ・ザ・イヤー（BBC Sports Personality of the Year）」は毎年12月に授与される賞です。メインである「BBCスポーツ・パーソナリティ・オブ・ザ・イヤー賞」にはスポーツで活躍した個人が選ばれ、2020年はF1レーサーのルイス・ハミルトン（Lewis Hamilton, 1985- ）が2014年に続き2度目の受賞を果たしました。1954年の開始当初、賞は1つだけでしたが、徐々に他の賞が加えられ、現在は様々な賞があります。「BBCスポーツ・名もなき英雄賞」は2003年に始められた賞で、人々のスポーツへの参加をボランティアで手助けしながらも、その功績がまだ知られていない人物に与えられます。BBCの15の地方局がそれぞれ1人ずつ地域での受賞者を選び、その中から名もなき英雄賞が選ばれます。ニュースの中のオードリー・リヴィングストンはトライアスロンにおける功績が讃えられ、2020年にBBCロンドンより選出されました。

　トライアスロンとは、水泳、自転車ロードレース、長距離走を1人で行う耐久競技です。イギリスでは1983年にレディングで初めてレースが行われて以来競技人口が年々増加しており、2019年には15万人に達しました。トライアスロン・イングランド（Triathlon England）、トライアスロン・スコットランド（Triathlon Scotland）、ウェルシュ・トライアスロン（Welsh Triathlon）の会員の合計は2009年からの10年間で3倍となり、2019年には3万3,000人が会員登録をしています。

　トライアスロンへの参加者の数が年々増加するにつれ、女性の参加者もイギリスでは2013年の26%から、2019年には32%へと徐々に増えています。しかし、トライアスロンの競技人口における黒人、アジア人などのマイノリティの割合はわずか2%に留まっています。リヴィングストンが2006年にトライアスロンを始めた当初はまだ競技者に白人男性が多い時代でしたが、ここ数年で少しずつ多様化が進みつつあります。イギリスにおける黒人やアジア人女性の中には、水泳やスポーツへの参加に障壁を感じている人が数多くいますが、そのようなマイノリティの女性が水泳に参加する手助けをするべく、リヴィングストンは2020年にソウル・スイマーズUK（Soul Swimmers UK）を立ち上げました。また、2020年10月の黒人歴史月間（Black History Month）にはトライアスロンと人種について語るなど、トライアスロンにおける多様性を目指して積極的に活動を行っています。

参考：
https://www.bbc.co.uk/programmes/b00grqnh
https://www.britishtriathlon.org

5 Filling Gaps | News Story

▶ Watch the news, then fill the gaps in the text.

Newsreader: Next weekend the BBC will reflect on a sporting year like no other, at the BBC Sports Personality Awards (¹   ). Among those being (²   ) are unsung heroes from every part of the UK, including one woman from the capital who's worked tirelessly to encourage more people into the sports of triathlon and swimming. Chris Slegg has her story.

Chris Slegg: Audrey Livingston didn't take up triathlon until she was (³   ) (⁴   ) (⁵   ). She loved it so much, she gave up her job in ₁₀ advertising, and (⁶   ) as a coach.

Audrey Livingston: Keeping that back leg straight ...

Slegg: She has since (⁷   ) dozens of people at Crystal Palace Triathlon Club, and Windrush Triathlon Club, to get (⁸   ) in the sport.

Livingston: When I was in advertising sales, the reward was you get a ₁₅ (⁹   ) at the end of the month, like "Yay!" Um, whereas my reward isn't money. You can't (¹⁰   ) it, it's people, saying, "Oh my god, I'm feeling so much better!", or "Oh god, I've lost so much (¹¹   )!"

First woman: I've known Audrey for nearly 10 years. Audrey has been my personal coach, and she has helped me (¹²   ) my goals. ₂₀

Livingston: Go ...

Slegg: Audrey has also set up Soul Swimmers, to try to (¹³   ) more black women to try swimming.

Second woman: She is one of those people, she's just hands-on, she just does it.

Man: Audrey came up with a brilliant idea of (¹⁴   ) training during the ₂₅ pandemic, where she coaches a group of people (¹⁵   ) over an audio link, and gives you instructions over headphones.

Slegg: We hadn't told Audrey why we were (¹⁶   ) until ...

Third woman: Have you heard of something called the BBC Unsung Hero Award? ₃₀

Livingston: Yeah.

Third woman: Ok, how would you feel if I told you that you'd won?

Livingston: No! ... Have I? ... No! Oh ... Wow!

Fourth woman: Audrey thoroughly deserves this award. Congratulations, Audrey!

Fifth woman: Thanks Audrey, for being such an (**17**   ) to the young people of South London.

Livingston: Thank you, London.

Slegg: Audrey Livingston – a true sporting (**18**   ) hero. Chris Slegg, BBC London.

35

40

(Monday 14 December 2020)

Notes

l.3 **the BBC Sports Personality (of the Year) Awards**「BBCスポーツ・パーソナリティ（オブ・ザ・イヤー）賞」イギリス国内における全スポーツの最優秀選手に贈られる賞。一般の投票によって選ばれる。1954年より、毎年12月に授与されている　l.13 **Crystal Palace Triathlon Club**「クリスタル・パレス・トライアスロン・クラブ」ロンドン南東部クリスタル・パレスにあるトライアスロン・クラブ。1993年創設　l.14 **Windrush Triathlon Club**「ウィンドラッシュ・トライアスロン・クラブ」ロンドン南東部ブリクストンにあるトライアスロン・クラブ。2008年創設　l.31 **the BBC (Sports) Unsung Hero Award**「BBC（スポーツ）名もなき英雄賞」

様々な混合競技

「トライアスロン (triathlon)」は、ギリシャ語で「3」を表す接頭辞 tri- と、「競技」を表す athlon とを組み合わせたもので、水泳、自転車ロードレース、長距離走の３種目を行うことからこのように呼ばれています。スポーツ界には、他にも数を表す接頭辞を語源に持つ様々な競技があります。「バイアスロン (biathlon)」はラテン語で「2」を表す bi- と athlon を組み合わせた競技で、クロスカントリースキーとライフル射撃の２種目を行います。４つの種目を合わせた「クアドラスロン (quadrathlon)」では水泳、自転車ロードレース、カヤック、長距離走を行い、5種目の「ペンタスロン (pentathlon)」では射撃、水泳、フェンシング、馬術、長距離走を行います。10種の「デカスロン (decathlon)」、20種の「アイコサスロン (icosathlon)」などもあり、どれも１人のアスリートが複数の種目で競い合う混成競技です。

Moving On

6 Making a Summary

 CD1-04

▶ Fill the gaps to complete the summary.

One of the annual BBC Sports Personality Awards is the (U   ) Hero Award, for people who have done a great job for sport without financial reward or even much recognition. The Award for the London region in 2020 was given to Audrey Livingston, for working (t   ) to encourage people into triathlon and swimming. In her forties, she gave up her job in advertising sales because the only reward was money, and (q   ) as a coach, where she is rewarded by people expressing their feelings, which cannot be (m   ). She has (i   ) dozens of people to get involved in triathlons and has also encouraged more black women to try swimming. During the pandemic she coached people (r   ) over an audio link, giving instructions over headphones. She helped people to (a   ) their goals and people thought she thoroughly deserved her award because she was an (i   ) to the people of South London.

7 Follow Up

▶ Discuss, write or present.

1. Think about why Audrey changed her job. Money wasn't important for her. Would you have felt the same way if you were her?

2. During the pandemic, Audrey started coaching people remotely, without actually seeing them. Would you like to be coached in that way? Would you be motivated?

3. Is there a similar award in Japan? Do you know of anybody who might deserve such an award?

Unit 2

Treasures of the Society of Antiquaries

近年イギリスで上昇し続ける家賃は、一般の人々だけでなく、数々の歴史的な品々を所蔵する学術機関にとっても大きな問題となっています。一体どのような問題なのでしょうか。ニュースを見てみましょう。

Starting Off

1 Setting the Scene

▶ What do you think?

1. Do you have a collection of old items that are important to you, that you want to save?
2. What museums have you been to? Did you enjoy your visit? How do you feel about them?
3. What is the purpose of museums? Do you think they are important?

2 Building Language

▶ Which word (1-6) best fits which explanation (a-f)?

1. heartbreaking [   ]   **a.** a contract you sign when you rent a property
2. repository   [   ]   **b.** provide funds so that an activity or company can carry on
3. lease   [   ]   **c.** a place where things can be stored safely
4. artifact   [   ]   **d.** a man-made object
5. existential   [   ]   **e.** related to whether you survive or not
6. subsidise   [   ]   **f.** extremely sad or sorrowful

Watching the News

3 Understanding Check 1

▶ Read the quotes, then watch the news and match them to the right people.

1. It runs contrary to everything that we as fellows, and this society stands for ...   [   ]

2. ... it's been home to some of the nation's most important historical treasures.   [   ]

3. Down here in the basement are all of the items that can't be on display ...   [   ]

4. We're that important.   [   ]

4 Understanding Check 2

▶ Which is the best answer?

1. What is the <u>main</u> purpose of the Society of Antiquaries?
   a. to store old objects that are too big for museums
   b. to help people understand the past
   c. to provide a space where the public can come and see treasures
   d. to buy and sell valuable artifacts

2. Which one of the following statements about the Society of Antiquaries is correct?
   a. They moved into New Burlington House 300 years ago, but now they cannot pay the rent.
   b. They have been in New Burlington House since the 1870s, but they don't own it.
   c. They bought New Burlington House in 2005, but won't pay for it until 2085.
   d. In six years, they must pay the government £3,000 rent.

3. Which <u>two</u> of the following plans did the second man mention?
   a. They want to have a place where the public can see the exhibits all year round.
   b. They are going to have special musical events to attract more people.
   c. They are thinking of rebuilding New Burlington House.
   d. They want to connect with schools and other educational establishments.

▶ **What do you remember?**

4. What examples were given of things stored by the Society of Antiquaries?

_____

5. If the Society of Antiquaries can't come to an agreement with the government, what will happen to its collection?

_____

6. What kind of solution are the government looking for?

_____

BACKGROUND INFORMATION

　ロンドン考古協会（The Society of Antiquaries）が1874年から入居しているバーリントン・ハウス（Burlington House）は、商業施設や高級ホテルが立ち並ぶロンドンの一等地、ウェスト・エンド地区のピカデリーにあります。元々はバーリントン伯爵家の私邸として17世紀半ばに建築されましたが、1854年にイギリス政府に購入されると様々な改装が行われ、複数の学会や協会が入居する学術振興の一大拠点となりました。

　バーリントン・ハウスの改装費と維持費は政府によって負担され、ロンドン考古協会をはじめとする各学術団体は当初、無料で建物を間借りすることが認められていました。ところが1990年代になって、非公式だったこれらの契約の法的根拠が議論されるようになり、2004年から2005年にかけて賃貸料を巡る裁判が行われました。結果として、ロンドン考古協会らは政府と賃借契約を結び、段階的に値上げしつつ80年後の2085年までに市場価値に見合った金額を支払うことで合意しました。しかし、2014年に政府の財政方針が転換されてバーリントン・ハウスが投資不動産として扱われるようになったこと、また、バーリントン・ハウスが建つウェスト・エンド地区の不動産価格が高騰し続けたことにより、2012年から13年には年間4,800ポンド（約67万円、1ポンド＝140円）だったロンドン考古協会が支払う賃貸料は、2018年から19年では年間15万ポンド（約2,100万円）まで跳ね上がりました。

　窮地に陥ったロンドン考古協会は賃料値上げに対抗するキャンペーンを2020年11月に開始し、一般の人々に対しても、国会議員に宛ててEメールを送ったり、ソーシャルメディアで周知したりといった方法での支援を呼びかけています。ロンドン考古協会によると、設立300周年となった2007年以来、協会は会員や学術関係者だけでなく一般の人々を対象とするプログラムにも力を入れており、公開講座や所蔵品の展示などを通じて公共の利益に貢献してきました。2019年の調査では、ロンドン考古協会が提供する公共的価値は年間540万ポンド（約7億5,600万円）近くに上るということで、協会は政府と一般の人々に対してその存在意義を訴え続けています。2021年3月にはロンドン地質学会とロンドン・リンネ協会もキャンペーンへの参加を表明しており、今後さらなる動きが加速する見込みです。

参考：
https://www.burlington.org.uk/archive/editorial/the-society-of-antiquaries
https://www.sal.org.uk/save-burlington-house/public-engagement-value/

---

5 Filling Gaps   News Story   CD1-05 [Original]   CD1-06 [Voiced]

▶ Watch the news, then fill the gaps in the text.

Newsreader: Now, for 300 years, it's been home to some of the nation's most important historical treasures. The Society of Antiquaries in Piccadilly was set up as an educational charity, to (¹   ) understanding of the past. But now, it says rent rises may force it to sell some of its (²

) collections, and the society says that would be (³   ). Caroline Davies has more.

Caroline Davies: In the heart of Piccadilly is New Burlington House, the home of the Society of Antiquaries.

Maurice Howard OBE, Former President, Society of Antiquaries: The society's been in (⁴   ) for 300 years. Before the National Gallery and the British Museum, we were the first (⁵   ) of the nation's past. We're that important.

Davies: Among the society's (⁶   ) are several copies of the Magna Carta, a cross found on the field at the Battle of Bosworth, medieval illustrated (⁷   ), and an ornamental shield from the Bronze Age.

Davies: New Burlington House was built for the society in the 1870s, but it's owned by the government. In 2005, they signed a (⁸   ) agreeing to pay market value rent by 2085. But the society say the government has dramatically (⁹   ) the rent already, by over 3,000% in six years.

Davies: Down here in the basement are all of the items that can't be on display in the rest of the building. There are 140,000 items in the library and 40,000 (¹⁰   ). But the society say that if they don't come to an (¹¹   ) with the government on rent, that some of them might need to be sold.

John Lewis, Secretary and Chief Executive, Society of Antiquaries: The thought of having to start breaking our collection up, um, is (¹²   ) for us. It runs contrary to everything that we as fellows, and this society stands for, and yet we are facing an absolutely (¹³   ) threat.

Davies: New Burlington House is an expensive address, and the society is currently paying

30% of market rent. Its (**14**   ) aren't currently open to the public, apart from their summer exhibitions, or for academics. Given that, why should it be (**15**   )?

Lewis: We do have plans to, to, to change the building, to have a (**16**   ) exhibition space, to, er, make it more interpretation ... to have an educational (**17**   ) programme.

Davies: The government say that they are (**18**   ) to the society's position, and are exploring whether there's a solution that can deliver value for (**19**   ), and help the societies to remain at New Burlington House. After this year, demands for government (**20**   ) are many. But the society are hoping some solution can be found, to keep them in their historic home. Carolyn Davies, BBC London.   *(Friday 15 January 2021)*

Notes

l.3 **The Society of Antiquaries**「ロンドン考古協会」イギリスの骨董と歴史に関する学問と知識への奨励・促進・助成を目的とした学術機関。1707年設立 　l.4 **Piccadilly**「ピカデリー」ロンドン中心部にある通りの名前で、繁華街として知られている 　l.9 **New Burlington House**「ニュー・バーリントン・ハウス」ロンドンのピカデリーにある建築物。1854年にイギリス政府がバーリントン・ハウスを購入後、1873年に新たな建物であるニュー・バーリントン・ハウスが増築された。現在はロンドン考古協会の他にロイヤル・アカデミー・オブ・アーツ（Royal Academy of Arts）、ロンドン地質学会（Geological Society of London）、ロンドン・リンネ協会（Linnean Society of London）、王立天文学会（Royal Astronomical Society）、王立化学会（Royal Society of Chemistry）の6団体がバーリントン・ハウスを使用している 　l.11 **OBE**（=Officer of the Order of the British Empire）「大英帝国勲章将校」イギリスの騎士団勲章である大英帝国勲章（the Order of the British Empire）のうち四等勲位にあたり、受賞者は名前の後に勲位を付けることが許可されている。1917年にジョージ5世（George V, 1865-1936）が創設 　l.12 **the National Gallery**「ナショナル・ギャラリー」ロンドンのトラファルガー広場にある美術館。1824年設立 　l.12 **the British Museum**「大英博物館」ロンドンのブルームズベリーにある博物館。1753年設立 　l.15 **the Magna Carta**「マグナ・カルタ（大憲章）」イングランド王国で1215年、ジョン王の時代に制定された憲章。国王権濫用の制限、民の権利や自由の保証などが記され、イギリス憲法の基礎となった。ロンドン考古協会は1215年の勅許状の草稿と1225年の改正版2つの計3つの文書を所蔵している 　l.16 **the Battle of Bosworth**「ボズワースの戦い」1485年に起こった、イングランド王国ヨーク朝のリチャード3世と後の王ヘンリー7世の間の戦い。リチャード3世の戦死とヘンリー7世によるテューダー朝の樹立で幕を閉じ、長く続いた薔薇戦争に終結をもたらした。1778年にボズワースの戦場で発見されたとされている十字架は、1881年にロンドン考古協会へ寄贈された 　l.17 **the Bronze Age**「青銅器時代」石器時代（Stone Age）と鉄器時代（Iron Age）の間の、青銅器が多く用いられた時代で、年代は地域によって異なる。1779年、スコットランドのエアシャー（Ayrshire）にある町ビース（Beith）で発見された青銅器時代の盾は、青銅器時代後期の紀元前1300年から1100年のものと考えられ、1791年にロンドン考古協会へ寄贈された

ケルムズコット・マナー

ロンドン考古協会が所有・管理している珠玉の歴史的建造物がケルムズコット・マナー（Kelmscott Manor）です。コッツウォルズ地方に位置するかつての荘園領主の邸宅は、この地域固有のハチミツ色の石灰石で統一され、最古の部分は 1570 年頃、地元の農園主トマス・ターナー（Thomas Turner）によって建てられました。その後代々増築しながら受け継がれ、ジェイムズ・ターナー（James Turner, d. 1870）の代で荘園となり、ケルムズコット・マナーと命名されました。1871 年には、アーツ・アンド・クラフツ運動（Arts and Crafts Movement）の指導者で、作家、デザイナー、社会主義者のウィリアム・モリス（William Morris, 1834-1896）の所有となり、彼にとっての憩いの場であり発想の源となりました。庭園に設置されたドラゴンのトピアリーは、北欧神話に造詣の深いモリスが最初に剪定したもので、今でも維持されています。また、邸内に設置された印刷所では、中世の写本を模してデザインされた希少本が作られ、貴重な美術品として世界中で大切にされています。

Moving On

6 Making a Summary

CD1-07

▶ Fill the gaps to complete the summary.

The Society of Antiquaries was set up 300 years ago to promote understanding of the past. Its home, New Burlington House, in Piccadilly, is a (r   ) for 140,000 items and 40,000 (a   ), including copies of the Magna Carta and a shield from the Bronze Age. They moved there in the 1870s, but it belongs to the government. In 2005, they signed a (l   ), agreeing to pay market rent by 2085, but the rent has increased by 3,000% in six years. This is an (e   ) threat, as in order to pay this, they might have to break up their collection, which would be (h   ). The government want a solution that will deliver (v   ) for taxpayers, who might not want to (s   ) a society whose treasures are not open to the public. However, the society are planning to have a permanent exhibition space, and an educational (o   ) programme.

7 Follow Up

▶ Discuss, write or present.

1. Do you think that the taxpayer should subsidise an organisation like the Society of Antiquaries? Does it deliver value to the public?

2. Are there any places or organisations like the Society of Antiquaries in Japan?

3. The Society of Antiquaries believes that its collection of artifacts can provide an understanding of the past. Do you agree? Make a list of objects from the 2020s that will help people of the future understand the Japan of today.

Unit 3

Changing Careers in the Pandemic

新型コロナウイルスの流行による社会や経済の変化は、若者の働き方にも影響を与えています。若者たちはこの状況をどのように乗り越えようとしているのでしょうか。ニュースを見てみましょう。

Starting Off

1 Setting the Scene

▶ What do you think?

1. How do you see your future career? Do you think you will keep the same career, or perhaps change one day?
2. Has the COVID-19 pandemic changed your life? If so, what has changed most?
3. How easy is it these days to find a job that you like? In particular, how easy is it for young people?

2 Building Language

▶ Which word (1-6) best fits which explanation (a-f)?

1. havoc   [   ]   **a.** in control, understood, organised
2. innovate   [   ]   **b.** temporarily laid off from work
3. diversify   [   ]   **c.** chaos, destruction, confusion
4. furloughed   [   ]   **d.** introduce something new, or new ideas
5. sussed   [   ]   **e.** spread, create different forms of something
6. vulnerable   [   ]   **f.** at risk, in danger, capable of being damaged

3 Understanding Check 1

▶ Read the quotes, then watch the news and match them to the right people.

1. Some millennials have had no other choice but to press the pause button on their careers.   [   ]

2. And they've had this realisation that they need to make some money ...   [   ]

3. So, it's actually suiting people's lifestyles.   [   ]

4. ... having that time to really think about what it is I want, and what it is I enjoy the most.   [   ]

4 Understanding Check 2

▶ Which is the best answer?

1. Why have young people been rethinking their careers?
   a. They cannot afford to join an unpaid internship scheme.
   b. It is difficult to find jobs that they would usually do.
   c. If they work during the lockdown, they might catch the virus.
   d. Recruitment for some more interesting jobs has increased.

2. What made Cece leave her job in an advertising firm?
   a. She hated her job at the advertising firm.
   b. She was told that her job was going to end.
   c. She found a way to sell her paintings during lockdown.
   d. While she was working at home, she realised what she wanted to do.

3. In what way has 22-year-old Tom diversified his online recruitment platform?
   a. He has taken up farming.
   b. He wants to help the country, so he has become a fruit picker.
   c. He is finding fruit and vegetable pickers for farmers.
   d. He is connecting students with people who are on furlough.

4. What does history show the prospects for young people to be?

_____

5. In what way do Becky and Katie's virtual exercise classes suit people's lifestyles?

_____

6. What are under 25s using technology for?

_____

BACKGROUND INFORMATION

　2020年から始まった新型コロナウイルスの世界的流行は、イギリスの若者の人生にも多大な影響を与えました。16歳から24歳までの若者の雇用状況をウイルスの流行前後で比較すると、全体的に就業率の低下と失業率の増加が見られます。特に、2020年7月から9月までの期間における若者の失業率は、ウイルスが流行する前の水準に比べて15%も増加しました。その後、失業率は徐々に下がっているものの、就業率に関しては依然として低い状態が続いています。2021年1月から3月までの状況を2020年の同時期と比較すると、職に就いている若者の数は31万人減り、8%の減少となりました。また、若者の失業者は13,000人増え、2%の増加となっています。特に、24歳以下の若者の失業率は13.3%で、16歳以上の国民の失業率4.8%に比べて高くなっています。ウイルスの感染拡大防止のため、飲食や娯楽など若者が多く働いている業種が休業等を余儀なくされたことが要因とみられており、若者世代への打撃の深刻さが窺えます。

　企業による従業員解雇の拡大を防ぐため、イギリス政府は2020年3月に行ったロックダウン期間から「一時帰休制度（furlough system）」を導入しました。これは、従業員の給料の最大80%、月額では最大2,500ポンド（約35万円）までを政府が負担する制度で、2021年9月まで行われました。2021年1月末までに、政府は50億ポンド（約7兆円）以上を投じて約1,100万件の雇用維持を支援し、特に、飲食や宿泊などの接客業がこの制度を多く利用しました。24歳以下の若者世代では、2021年3月末の時点で、全対象件数の21%に相当する76万1,900件が利用しています。こうした政策や、コロナウイルスのワクチンが急速に普及したことにより、当初の見込みよりも低い失業率が維持されています。

　その一方で、転職を考える人の数も増えており、人々の仕事に対する意識は変化しつつあります。2021年4月に保険会社のアビバ（Aviva）が発表した調査では、イギリスの労働人口の60%が転職を考え、新しいスキルの習得や資格の取得を考慮していることがわかりました。とりわけ、若者世代では、転職を考えている人の割合は87%に上ります。また、在宅での仕事を希望する人や、趣味を仕事にしたいと考える人の割合も増えており、ウイルスの流行をきっかけとして、多くの人の生き方や考え方が変わりつつあります。

参考：
https://commonslibrary.parliament.uk/research-briefings/sn05871/
https://www.bbc.com/news/business-52660591
https://www.bbc.com/news/explainers-52135342

5 Filling Gaps | **News Story** | CD1-08 [Original] CD1-09 [Voiced]

▶ **Watch the news, then fill the gaps in the text.**

Newsreader: Well, we've been talking about the economic (¹   ) caused by this pandemic, but it's young people just starting out on their careers who are likely to be hardest hit. Across the world, companies have put a (²   ) on

5

recruitment or cancelled their internship schemes. But for some youngsters, a period in lockdown has (³   ) them to rethink their careers. Here's our business correspondent, Sarah Corker.

Katie Williams, boot camp instructor: Three, two, one, off you go ...   10

Sarah Corker: Fitness.

Williams: ... Claude, Emma, go for it ...

Corker: Farming.

Tom Bilborough, UniWrk: Most of our workers tend to be students.

Corker: And something far more (⁴   ).   15

Cece Philips, artist: I'm spending pretty much all my days now, um, just painting.

Corker: For these young people, the pandemic has taken their careers on a different (⁵   ).

Philips: I've gone from a large office in the middle of Soho to being at home, um, painting in my bedroom.   20

Corker: Last week Cece from London left her job at one of the world's largest advertising (⁶   ), to follow her artistic dreams.

Philips: I definitely don't think I would have made this (⁷   ), or made the jump, if it hadn't been for lockdown actually. Um, I've always loved art. I've always loved painting and drawing, and it was really actually working from home, being   25 in lockdown, and having that time to really think about what it is I want and what it is I enjoy the most.

Corker: History shows that young people may face years of reduced pay and limited job (⁸   ) long after this economic crisis has passed. Some millennials have had no other choice but to press the pause button on their careers. Others though, have adapted, (⁹   ), in some

30

unexpected ways.

Corker: Farming is one of the few industries still recruiting. In North Yorkshire, 22-year-old Tom has (**10**   ) his online recruitment platform. He's now connecting farmers with fruit and vegetable pickers.

Bilborough: And at the moment we're getting such a high demand from students, from people being (**11**   ), um, also from self-employed who are just sat at home now. And they've had this realisation that they need to make some money, and they'd love to help the country as well.

Williams: And down, all the way down and a big clap ...

Corker: And even the way we exercise has changed. Boot camp instructors Becky and Katie are running (**12**   ) classes on Zoom.

Williams: The first week, a bit (**13**   ), not great with technology, I'm not going to lie. So, um, there was a few like, little teething problems, but I've got it (**14**   ).

Corker: From their homes in Reading, they're (**15**   ) (**16**   ) with people from as far afield as Ireland and Canada.

Becky Hill, boot camp instructor: ... And rest, well done everyone.

Woman: Well done.

Corker: Do you think this is the fitness (**17**   ) changed forever?

Hill: A lot of our members are really happy that they can do five boot camps a week, as (**18**   ) to only being able to make it up to the field once or twice. So, it's actually suiting people's lifestyles.

Hill: Twenty seconds.

Corker: The under 25s may be the most financially (**19**   ) in this crisis but they're using technology to open up new (**20**   ) and now have more time to try out new strokes. Sarah Corker, BBC News.

(Thursday 14 May 2020)

パンデミックとパニック

　「パンデミック（pandemic）」という語はギリシア語の「パンデミア（pandemia）」が語源で、「全て（pan）」＋「人々（demos）」からなり、世界的流行を意味します。「パニック（panic）」という語は、「牧羊神パン（Pan）の性質をもった」というところから、「パンによって起こされた恐怖」が原義です。ギリシア神話の牧羊神パンは、森・野原・牧羊の神で、頭に角があり、耳と脚はヤギに似ていて、突然出現するために人間に恐れられていました。しかしイギリスの児童文学には、J. M. バリー（J. M. Barrie, 1860-1937）の造形したピーター・パンや、ケネス・グレアム（Kenneth Grahame, 1859-1932）の『たのしい川べ』（The Wind in the Willows, 1908）に登場するアシ笛を吹く牧神など、パンは愛すべきキャラクターとして登場しています。また、フランス印象派の作曲家クロード・ドビュッシー（Claude Debussy, 1862-1918）は、敬慕していた詩人ステファヌ・マラルメ（Stephane Mallarme, 1842-1898）の作品に感銘を受けて作曲した『「牧神の午後」への前奏曲』など、いくつかの作品で牧神をテーマにしています。

Moving On　　6 Making a Summary CD1-10

▶ Fill the gaps to complete the summary.

　The pandemic has caused economic (h　　　　), and the under 25s have been the most (v　　　　) group because companies have paused recruitment or cancelled internship schemes. They might face years of reduced pay and limited (p　　　　). However, this has prompted millennials to rethink their careers, and some of them have (a　　　　) and (i　　　　) in some unexpected ways. One woman quit her job in advertising when she realised after working at home that she loved art, and would rather be an artist. A young man, who runs an online recruitment platform, decided to (d　　　　). He is now connecting fruit and vegetable farmers with pickers. These new pickers are students, people being (f　　　　), or self-employed who need to make money and help the country. Finally, two women are running virtual boot camp classes on Zoom. They had a few (t　　　　) problems, but they got them (s　　　　), and it suits people's lifestyles as they can do five classes in a week. Young people are using (t　　　　) to open up new opportunities.

7 Follow Up

▶ Discuss, write or present.

1. What do you think of Cece's decision to quit her advertising job and become an artist? Was it wise? Is it the sort of decision that you could make?

2. It is possible to earn a lot by picking fruit and vegetables, but it's hard work. Would you like to do it? What if it is the only way for you to earn money?

3. Has the pandemic had a similar impact on young people in Japan? How easy is it to get a job? Do you know of any young people who have adapted, innovated, or diversified?

Unit 4

The Climate Change Threat to Heritage Sites

生態系への影響が懸念される気候変動ですが、思わぬところにも影を落とし始めているようです。人類の歴史や文化を脅かしつつある問題について、ニュースを見てみましょう。

Starting Off

1 Setting the Scene

▶ What do you think?

1. We all worry that climate change might cause damage in the future, but do you know of any damage that it has already caused?
2. Do you think it is important to look after and protect old buildings?
3. Do you know of any places that badly need repair? Do you think they will be repaired?

2 Building Language

▶ Which word (1-7) best fits which explanation (a-g)?

1. untouched   [   ]   a. easily damaged or affected
2. drought   [   ]   b. somebody who cares for or looks after something (or someone)
3. susceptible   [   ]   c. pouring or flowing fast, violently, or heavily
4. collapse   [   ]   d. a sudden, complete failure, breakdown, or destruction
5. torrential   [   ]   e. something that might be dangerous, or cause damage
6. threat   [   ]   f. not affected, changed, or damaged in any way
7. custodian   [   ]   g. a period of very dry weather, with not enough rain

3 Understanding Check 1

▶ Read the quotes, then watch the news and match them to the right people.

1. We have to take it seriously, and we have to respond accordingly.   [   ]

2. But Highgate Cemetery now faces damage and disease.   [   ]

3. ... so that variation has caused problems for the trees, and for us.   [   ]

4. The trees will be better looked after.   [   ]

4 Understanding Check 2

▶ Which is the best answer?

1. Which sentence contains the correct figures?
   a. 25,000 people are buried in the 36 acres of Highgate Cemetery. The project may take 170 years.
   b. 36,000 people are buried in the 170 acres of Highgate Cemetery. The project may take 25 years.
   c. 170,000 people are buried in the 25 acres of Highgate Cemetery. The project may take 36 years.
   d. 170,000 people are buried in the 36 acres of Highgate Cemetery. The project may take 25 years.

2. Which of the following was <u>not</u> mentioned as a cause of damage to trees?
   a. torrential rain
   b. drought
   c. extreme cold weather
   d. high winds

3. What might happen to the Tower of London?
   a. If we don't maintain the Thames Barrier, the Tower of London might be flooded.
   b. Like Hammersmith Bridge, the heat might cause cracks in the Tower to worsen.
   c. It might burn down, like the Notre Dame Cathedral, in France.
   d. Like the Palace of Westminster, the Tower might start to collapse.

▶ **What do you remember?**

4. What is Highgate Cemetery famous for? What threat are Highgate Cemetery and other London heritage sites facing?

_____

5. According to the man being interviewed, why should we plant the right trees in the right places?

_____

6. According to the woman at the end of the video, why must we take the threat of climate change seriously?

_____

BACKGROUND INFORMATION

　ハイゲート墓地は、ロンドンのシティ内の教会墓地が手狭になった1839年に開園しました。スティーブン・ギアリー（Stephen Geary, 1797-1854）によって設計された「エジプト風並木道（Egyptian Avenue）」と「テラス式地下埋葬所（Terrace Catacombs）」を含む西苑は、ヴィクトリア朝の「ゴシック復興様式（Gothic Revival）」を体現している一方、「牧夫の小径（Swain's Lane）」を挟んで1856年に拡張された東苑にはコンクリートとガラス製の現代建築の墓所もあり、現役の霊苑であることを意識させられます。開園当初は墓所参詣熱が高く、霊苑は都会のオアシスとして人気がありましたが、その後、訪問者は減少し、墓地は荒廃しました。しかし、1975年に「ハイゲート墓地フレンズ」が組織され、有志による保存活動が始まりました。近年、家系図作成の流行などとともに再び墓地の人気が高まり、2013年には6万3,000人だった有料入場者数が、2020年には10万人に増えました。非営利団体であるフレンズは、2つのコンペを実施し、墓地全体の概観を見直すと同時に、カフェやショップを開設して、観光客を呼び込む計画です。

　気候変動や海面上昇の影響は年々明らかになっており、洪水や山火事などが歴史的遺産に及ぼす脅威が懸念されています。ニュースでも言及されているハマースミス橋は、2019年、老朽化のため自動車の通行が、2020年には自転車や歩行者の通行も禁止となり、全面的に封鎖されました。調査によると、橋を吊り下げる支柱の鋳鉄に主に熱波が原因となって微細な亀裂が無数に走っており、突然崩壊する危険があることがわかりました。政府の補助を得て補修の計画が立てられましたが、人々の生活の一部となっている橋の閉鎖により、多大な影響が出ています。気候変動は各地で様々な影響を及ぼしており、イングリッシュ・ヘリテッジやナショナル・トラスト（National Trust）など文化遺産や自然遺産の保護に従事する団体は、科学者や様々な団体と連携し、調査や対策に力を尽くしています。

参考：
https://archaeology-travel.com/england/highgate-cemetery-london/
https://historicengland.org.uk/whats-new/statements/climate-change/

5 Filling Gaps | News Story | ⊙ CD1-11-[Original] ⊙ CD1-12-[Voiced]

▶ **Watch the news, then fill the gaps in the text.**

Newsreader: Now, it's known for its (¹   ) woodland and the graves of famous Londoners, including Karl Marx and George Michael. But Highgate Cemetery now faces damage and disease. And it's not the only heritage site in the capital facing a (²   ) from our climate change, as our environment correspondent, Tom Edwards, reports.

Tom Edwards: Highgate Cemetery in North London. Thirty-six acres in size, where 170,000 Londoners are (³   ). Well-known for its romantic decay, but here nature is now starting to (⁴   ) real problems.

April Cameron, horticulturist: You can see the cracking on the trunk, and that's probably as a result of, um, (⁵   ). And then the cracks are entry points for fungal (⁶   ).

Edwards: Trees here are now getting stressed. (⁷   ) heat, flooding, high winds, are making them much more (⁸   ) to disease, and the (⁹   ) onto graves.

Cameron: Partly it's the age of the trees, but that (¹⁰   ) with climate change has put them under stress. We've had some very dry summers here, and the ground conditions have been very dry for these trees. Then we maybe have had (¹¹   ) rain, so that variation has caused problems for the trees, and for us.

Dr. Ian Dungavell, Chief Executive of Friends of Highgate Cemetery: And there's another one down the path here where it's cracked a headstone in two ...

Edwards: Here they've started an (¹²   ) competition. They want to rethink the cemetery, and perhaps replant some trees, more (¹³   ) to a changing climate.

Dungavell: The trees will be better looked after. We'll have the right variety of trees, planted in the right places, and some of that will be for (¹⁴   ) reasons, to create a different variety of habitats, and some of it will be for (¹⁵   ) reasons.

Edwards: Climate change according to English Heritage is one of the most significant and fastest growing (¹⁶   ) to cultural heritage. And it says early action is now needed to build in safeguards to try and (¹⁷   ) it.

Edwards: At Hammersmith Bridge, cracks (¹⁸   ) due to the heat this summer. And experts say other historic buildings like the Palace of Westminster, or the Tower of London could also be (¹⁹   ) to flooding, if the Thames Barrier isn't kept effective.

Professor May Cassar, University College London: The science is secure. The (²⁰   ) is there. We have to take it seriously, and we have to respond accordingly. And I think we would be irresponsible heritage guardians and (²¹   ) if we did not. And I do not know of one heritage organisation that is not taking this (²²   ) seriously.

Edwards: This project in Highgate could take 25 years. Part of London's historic and cultural sites, trying to protect themselves against the changing climate. Tom Edwards, BBC London.

(Friday 11 December 2020)

Notes

l.3 **Karl Marx**「カール・マルクス (1818-83)」ドイツ出身の経済学者かつ哲学者。1849年にイギリスに渡った。著書『資本論』(*Capital: Critique of Political Economy*, 1867) で知られる　l.4 **George Michael**「ジョージ・マイケル (1963-2016)」イギリスのシンガーソングライター。アンドリュー・リッジリー (Andrew Ridgeley, 1963-) と共に、ポップデュオのワム！(Wham!) として活躍した　l.4 **Highgate Cemetery**「ハイゲート墓地」ロンドン北部の高級住宅街ハイゲートにある墓地。1839年開園　l.23 **Friends of Highgate Cemetery**「ハイゲート墓地フレンズ」ハイゲート墓地の保全活動を行っている慈善団体。1975年設立　l.35 **English Heritage**「イングリッシュ・ヘリテッジ」イングランドの歴史的建造物や記念物を保存し維持するための組織。1983年に設立された政府機関を前身とする　l.41 **Hammersmith Bridge**「ハマースミス橋」ロンドン西部にある、テムズ川に架かる吊り橋。1827年開通。2019年、老朽化のため自動車の通行が禁止となった。2020年には自転車や歩行者の通行も禁止となって、全面的に封鎖された　l.43 **the Palace of Westminster**「ウェストミンスター宮殿」ロンドン中心部のシティ・オブ・ウェストミンスターにある宮殿で、国会議事堂として使用されている。テムズ川沿いに建つ。最初の宮殿は11世紀に建設されたが、1834年に火事で焼失した。現在ある建物はその後再建されたもの　l.43 **the Tower of London**「ロンドン塔」イースト・ロンドンに建つ城塞。テムズ川沿いにある。11世紀に建てられ、監獄や処刑場としても使用された　l.44 **the Thames Barrier**「テムズバリア」テムズ川に建設された可動式防潮堤。全長520メートル。ロンドン東部のウーリッジ近くに設置され、テムズ川の氾濫から街を守る役割を持つ。1984年に正式に運用が開始された

ハイゲート・ヴァンパイア

　1970年、ハイゲート墓地にヴァンパイアがいるという噂がセンセーションを巻き起こしました。事の発端はデイヴィッド・ファラント（David Farrant）という人物が墓地で幽霊のような姿に遭遇し、2月6日発行の地元紙で他にも見た人がいないか尋ねたことでした。すると27日の同紙でショーン・マンチェスター（Sean Manchester）という人が、それはヴァンパイアの王であると主張し始めます。二人とも悪魔祓いが出来ると言い張り、お互いの方法を激しく批判し合いました。同年3月、不吉な日とされる13日の金曜日に、テレビ局のITVがヴァンパイア狩りをするという両者の取材を行いました。その様子が夕方に放送されると、群衆がロンドン内外から墓地に押し寄せ、閉ざされた門や壁によじ登り、警察が出動する大事態になりました。お互いを罵り合ったファラントとマンチェスターのライバル関係は、2019年にファラントが亡くなるまで続きました。

Moving On

6 Making a Summary

 CD1-13

▶ Fill the gaps to complete the summary.

　Highgate Cemetery is famous for its (u　　　　　　　) woodland and romantic (d　　　　　　　). However, like a lot of well-known (h　　　　　　) sites in London, it is facing a (t　　　　　　) from climate change and extreme weather. In particular, (d　　　　　　), extreme heat, and floods from (t　　　　　　) rain have put the trees under stress and made them (s　　　　　　) to disease and caused them to (c　　　　　　) onto graves. There is a plan to replant with a variety of trees more suitable to the changing climate, not only to provide a variety of habitats, but also for (a　　　　　　) reasons. Other London (h　　　　　　) sites are also at risk, with some historic buildings, like the Tower of London, (s　　　　　　) to flooding. According to Professor May Cassar, there is strong evidence of the (t　　　　　　), so we would be irresponsible (c　　　　　　) of our (h　　　　　　) if we did not respond seriously.

7 Follow Up

▶ Discuss, write or present.

1. Of course, there are lots of heritage sites in Japan, but are there any sites similar to Highgate Cemetery?

2. Can you think of any examples where a Japanese heritage site has been repaired, to bring it back to good condition?

3. We discussed the damage from climate change at the start of the unit. However, do you think it is right to prioritise heritage sites? Are there more important places that we should spend money to protect or repair?

Plastic from Peas

化粧品や洗剤などに含まれるマイクロプラスチックが環境を汚染し、食物連鎖に悪影響を与えています。地球に優しいプラスチックは実現可能でしょうか。ある取り組みを見てみましょう。

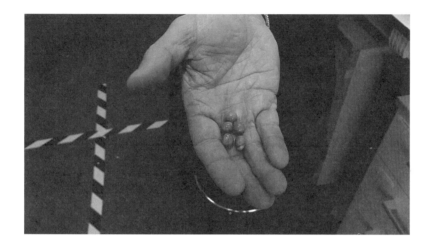

Starting Off

1 Setting the Scene

▶ What do you think?

1. Think of all the things that you use in daily life. How many of them are made of plastic?
2. Make a list of all those plastic items that you use only once and then throw away.
3. Do you think that all the plastic that you throw away harms our environment?

2 Building Language

▶ For each word (1-6), find two synonyms (a-l).

1. fragrance   [   ][   ]
2. engineer   [   ][   ]
3. degrade   [   ][   ]
4. perfect   [   ][   ]
5. swap   [   ][   ]
6. ban   [   ][   ]

a. substitute   g. proscribe
b. fabricate   h. improve
c. reconstruct   i. refine
d. smell   j. deteriorate
e. prohibit   k. exchange
f. decompose   l. perfume

Watching the News

3 Understanding Check 1

▶ Read the quotes, then watch the news and match them to the right people.

1. So, after the coating has been dried in the oven, it turns into a lovely film ...   [   ]

2. There's something very wrong about making materials from, er, oil that last just for a minute or two.   [   ]

3. Very nice! It's hard to eat an apple nicely on camera.   [   ]

4. Now, many of us are aware of the environmental dangers of microplastics ...   [   ]

4 Understanding Check 2

▶ Which is the best answer?

1. Why don't their lab coats smell bad?
   a. They are not made of plastic.
   b. They contain very small plastic balls that smell nice.
   c. They always get washed into the environment.
   d. They keep them for decades.

2. Which of the following statements is correct?
   a. Peas are not the only plant they can use to make plastic.
   b. It takes 15 years to make plastic from peas.
   c. Potatoes cannot be used, because they need something that comes out as a liquid.
   d. Only potatoes can be made into plastic-like sheets.

3. What single-use plastic product was <u>not</u> mentioned by the reporter?
   a. dishwasher tablets
   b. coffee cups
   c. sandwich packets
   d. sweet wrappers

26

4. What 'first' has this company achieved?

_____

5. What danger about this new process did the the reporter ask about?

_____

6. What was the last man's answer to the reporter's question above about danger?

_____

BACKGROUND INFORMATION

　マイクロプラスチックが近年問題になっていますが、その種類にはマイクロビーズやマイクロカプセルなどがあります。マイクロビーズとはプラスチックで作られた微粒子のことで、研磨などの目的で洗顔料、石鹸、歯磨き粉、化粧品などの製品に用いられています。マイクロビーズは微細であるため、洗い流されてそのまま川や海に流れ込み、環境汚染や食物連鎖によって人体に深刻な影響を与えるリスクが指摘されています。2018年1月9日、イギリス環境・食糧・農村地域省（DEFRA: Department for Environment, Food & Rural Affairs）はマイクロビーズを含む製品の製造を禁止しました。同年6月19日には、マイクロビーズが使われている化粧品やパーソナルケア製品の販売がイングランドとスコットランドで禁止され、その後ウェールズと北アイルランドにも拡大されました。しかし、柔軟剤、合成洗剤、芳香剤などに使用されている、香り成分をプラスチック粒子の中に閉じ込めたマイクロカプセルは、これらの禁止項目には含まれていません。この対策として2019年、EUの専門機関である欧州化学機関（ECHA: European Chemicals Agency）は、マイクロカプセルを含む、意図的に加えられたマイクロプラスチックの規制を提案しました。

　プラスチックによる環境汚染なしにマイクロプラスチックのメリットを享受できるという画期的な開発をしたエグザンプラ（Xampla）は2018年に設立され、世界で初めて植物性タンパク質からプラスチックの素材を製品化しました。これまでの植物由来のバイオプラスチックの多くは海藻や藻類でできていて、化学溶剤を加えることで強度や安定性を高めていたため、完全には自然分解されませんでした。しかし、エグザンプラが開発した製品は化学溶剤を加えないため、破棄されても自然の中で完全に素早く分解されるので、排水溝に流しても問題ありません。エグザンプラは、アミノ酸の自己組織化の能力を利用してタンパク質を成分とした糸を作り出す蜘蛛からインスピレーションを受け、蜘蛛が糸を作り出すのと同様のプロセスで植物性タンパク質からプラスチック素材を作り出す方法を発見しました。2021年、マイクロカプセルが先発商品として製品化され、その後この技術を応用したフィルムやコーティング製品の実用化に向けて動き出す予定です。この画期的な製品への期待は大きく、エグザンプラは2021年1月8日、新興企業への投資を行っている大手投資会社から6,200万ポンド（86億8,000万円）の資金調達を受ける契約を締結しました。

参考：

https://www.xampla.com/
https://echa.europa.eu/hot-topics/microplastics

5 Filling Gaps | News Story |

▶ **Watch the news, then fill the gaps in the text.**

Newsreader: Now, many of us are aware of the environmental dangers of microplastics, or microbeads, as millions of tons of them get washed into our seas and (¹   ). Well, now there's some good news. Based on work started at Cambridge University, a company's become the first in the world to make single-use plastic out of something that won't (²   ) the planet: peas. Here's our science correspondent, Richard Wescott.

5

Richard Wescott: Everyone in this lab is full of plastic. Well, their lab coats are anyway. A lot of our clothes are full of tiny little balls that have got (³   ) inside. It's what makes them smell so nice. Now, normally they're made of plastic, which washes into the environment and stays there for (⁴   ). What if you could make them out of something that's better for the planet, like peas?

10

Wescott: This is the first company in the world to (⁵   ) plant protein into a material that does the same job as single-use plastic. Things like the microcapsules that you'd often get inside fabric conditioners, or cosmetics.

15

Anne Jacobs, biochemist, Xampla: At the moment the microcapsules contain plastic which would not (⁶   ) and last for ages in the ocean. Our capsules were made of protein and would be eaten by fish eventually.

20

Wescott: It's taken 15 years to (⁷   ) the process. Here, they're using peas, but you can use other (⁸   ) plants including potatoes. Eventually, it comes out as a liquid, that can be made into plastic-like sheets.

Polly Keen, chemical engineer, Xampla: So, after the coating has been dried in the oven, it turns into a lovely film, which we can then turn into a (⁹   ) like that that's on your apple there.

25

Wescott: So basically that's the equivalent of a plastic (¹⁰   ), but I can eat it.

Keen: Yes, it's ...

Wescott: You (¹¹   )?

30

Keen: ... just 100% pea protein.

Wescott: Okay. Very nice! It's hard to eat an apple nicely on camera.

28

Wescott: Dishwasher tablets, sandwich packets, sweet wrappers. All made of something that (¹²   ) naturally, in a matter of days.

Wescott: Is there a danger you're just (¹³   ) one problem with another? So, farmers who should be growing food are actually going to grow peas to make plastic, and then we don't have enough food?

Simon Hombersley, CEO, Xampla: There are a lot of (¹⁴   ) products already in the farming process that have got very low value, or even are just (¹⁵   ) straight back into the field, that can be sold on and used to, to make our kind of materials. Single-use plastics, and microplastics don't need to be made from (¹⁶   ) fuels. There's something very wrong about making materials from, er, oil that last just for a minute or two.

Wescott: It's thought the average family washes around 14 million tiny plastic balls down the (¹⁷   ) each week. Several countries are in the process of (¹⁸   ) them. Now, there's a way of (¹⁹   ) that harmful plastic for something made from peas. Richard Wescott, BBC News, Cambridge.

(Wednesday 16 September 2020)

Notes

l.6 **Cambridge University**「ケンブリッジ大学」イングランドのケンブリッジにある大学。オックスフォード大学と共に伝統を誇り、その歴史は13世紀にさかのぼる　l.18 **Xampla**「エグザンプラ」ケンブリッジ大学の研究室から2018年に独立した会社

BEHIND THE SCENES

「あつあつ豆がゆ」

　豆は昔からイギリス人の食生活に欠かせないもので、18世紀のマザーグースにも「あつあつ豆が
ゆ」("Pease Porridge Hot", c. 1760) という童謡があります。タイトルにあるpeaseとはエンド
ウマメを表す中英語で、元は単数形および形容詞形であったものを複数形と誤認したことから、現在
使われているpeaという単語が生まれました。軽快なライムを持つこの童謡は、日本の「せっせっせ」
のように2人1組で行われる手遊び歌で、冬の寒い晩などには体を温めるのによく遊ばれたと言われ
ています。ちなみに、歌詞に出てくる「熱いのが好きな人もいれば、冷めたのが好きな人もいる
(Some like it hot, some like it cold)」という箇所は、アメリカの女優マリリン・モンロー (Marilyn
Monroe, 1926-62) 主演の映画『お熱いのがお好き』(*Some Like It Hot*, 1959) のタイトルに引
用されています。

Moving On

6 Making a Summary

▶ Fill the gaps to complete the summary.

　The single-use plastic that we throw away everyday damages the environment. For
example, our clothes contain tiny plastic microcapsules, which contain (f　　　　　).
Each week, the average family washes about 14 million of these tiny balls out into the
sea, where they stay for decades. Some countries are going to (b　　　　　) them.
However, we can (s　　　　　) that harmful plastic for something made from peas.
One company has taken 15 years to (p　　　　　) a process to make microcapsules
and other plastic items that can (d　　　　　) naturally in days, and eventually be
eaten by fish. They have created this material by (e　　　　　) plant protein from
peas and other plants. Richard Wescott wondered whether we might not have enough
food if farmers sell their peas for plastic, but the CEO replied that we could use waste
products which now are just (p　　　　　) back into the field.

7 Follow Up

▶ Discuss, write or present.

1. How important do you think this invention is? The company has spent 15 years
   perfecting the process, but are there more important problems they should be trying
   to solve?

2. Do you think we could solve the problem by just using less plastic? Why, for example,
   are they in cosmetics? Are they really necessary?

3. Do you agree with Wescott that we need to be careful that farmers should focus on
   growing food instead of selling their crop to make plastic?

Unit 6

Return of the Red Kites

街中で、ある動物による被害が相次いでいます。人間の生活を守りつつ、動物と共存していくことは可能なのでしょうか。ニュースを見てみましょう。

Starting Off

1 Setting the Scene

▶ What do you think?

1. How many different types of birds can you think of? (The Japanese name is fine if you don't know the English name.) Describe them.
2. Do you have any favourite birds? Why do you like them?
3. Are there any birds that cause problems?

2 Building Language

▶ Which word (1-8) best fits which explanation (a-h)?

1. scavenge   [   ]   a. too dependent on something
2. tolerate   [   ]   b. suddenly dive fast through the air
3. carrion   [   ]   c. permit something distasteful without objection
4. over-reliant   [   ]   d. existing and seen in many places
5. ubiquitous   [   ]   e. separate and move away in different directions
6. swoop   [   ]   f. gather and crowd together in one place
7. disperse   [   ]   g. decaying flesh of dead animals
8. cluster   [   ]   h. search for something edible or usable from dead or unwanted material

Watching the News

3 Understanding Check 1

▶ Read the quotes, then watch the news and match them to the right people.

1. So, we'd really urge people not to put food out for them.   [   ]
2. And, specifically it was the red kite he was talking about.   [   ]
3. However, they're now a familiar sight in and around the Chilterns …

          [   ]
4. Something whooshed past my head.

          [   ]

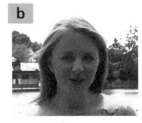

4 Understanding Check 2

▶ Which is the best answer?

1. Why was the mother surprised when she went to the doctors?
   a. She found out that it was more serious than she thought because it was caused by a wild animal.
   b. She was told that red kites are endangered, so this happens very rarely.
   c. Her son had a small scratch, which she found out wasn't common.
   d. She found out that a similar incident had happened half an hour earlier.

2. Which of the following sentences is correct, according to the video?
   a. A hundred years ago, red kites were almost extinct, but today there are 1,800 breeding pairs in the UK.
   b. In the late 1980s, there were 1,800 breeding pairs in the UK, but today they are almost extinct.
   c. Thanks to the careful collection of eggs, red kites are one of Britain's greatest conservation successes.
   d. Red kites were deliberately poisoned in the 1980s, so now there are only 1,800 remaining.

3. Which of the following sentences is correct, according to the video?
   a. The birds are dispersing across the UK, which was the original intention.
   b. The petition is asking people to leave food for the birds.
   c. Because they are being fed artificially, the birds will not cluster.
   d. The birds are behaving in an unnatural way.

4. Why are people in the area being asked to help?

_____

5. Why were red kites useful in the days of Shakespeare?

_____

6. What does the future of these birds depend on?

_____

BACKGROUND INFORMATION

　2006年1月、ロンドンでアカトビが目撃されましたが、それは1859年以来およそ150年ぶりのことでした。しかし、文豪シェイクスピア（William Shakespeare, 1564-1616）は、戯曲『コリオレイナス』（*Coriolanus*, 1608）の中で、ロンドンを「トビとカラスの街」と形容しており、また、『冬物語』（*Winter's Tale*, 1611）においても、トビの巣作りの季節には洗濯物に気をつけるよう警告する台詞があります。17世紀当時のロンドンでは、ロンドン塔の守護鳥とされる大鴉と同じくらいアカトビが生息しており、動物の死骸や人間の出すゴミの処理に役立っていました。しかし、公衆衛生の向上と共にその数は減り、18世紀末にはロンドン市内で繁殖するつがいはいなくなりました。イギリス全土でもその数は減少していましたが、1903 年にその存続を危惧する有志によって保護委員会が結成され、1905年以来英国鳥類保護協会（RSPB: the Royal Society for the Protection of Birds）がその保護に関わってきました。アカトビの数は一時期急速に減少し、ウェールズに少数の個体が生息するのみとなりました。その珍しさゆえに卵や個体が賞金稼ぎに狙われ、1980年代にはイギリス国内では絶滅危惧種に指定されました。

　1986年、英国鳥類保護協会と自然保護協会（NCC: Nature Conservancy Council）の協議の結果、イングランドとスコットランドにアカトビを再移入させることとなりました。種の再移入は国際自然保護連合（IUCN: International Union for the Conservation of Nature）の厳しい審査基準に見合わなければなりません。審査を通過したアカトビは、1989年のウェールズとスウェーデンからの数羽を皮切りに、1994年までにイングランドとスコットランドの2ヶ所の地点に93羽ずつ、スウェーデンとスペインから移入されました。その後も数ヶ所の地点に、イギリス国内やドイツなどから移入が行われました。アカトビの再移入は20世紀の最も成功した動物保護活動となりました。イングランドでの移入地点に採用されたチルターン丘陵（the Chiltern Hills）では、戻ってきたアカトビの優雅な飛翔が観光の呼び物ともなっていますが、問題も生じています。アカトビとの共生のために、餌付けを控えるなど人々のマナーが問われています。

参考：
https://www.theguardian.com/environment/2021/may/25/red-kite-attacks-why-birds-of-prey-are-causing-havoc-on-the-streets-of-henley
https://www.chilternsaonb.org/about-chilterns/red-kites.html
https://www.rspb.org.uk/birds-and-wildlife/wildlife-guides/bird-a-z/red-kite/

5 Filling Gaps | News Story

CD1-17 [Original] CD1-18 [Voiced]

▶ **Watch the news, then fill the gaps in the text.**

Newsreader: Now, they were once considered
(**1**   ). However, they're now a
familiar sight in and around the Chilterns,
after being reintroduced into the area
around three decades ago. But there are
concerns that this bird of prey, which largely
(**2**   ) its food, is becoming (**3**   ) on food handouts.
Now people in the area are being asked to help, as Wendy Hurrell explains.

Wendy Hurrell: It was William Shakespeare who, in one of his plays, described London
as the city of kites and crows. And, specifically it was the red kite he was talking
about.

Hurrell: They were more than (**4**   ). Because they feed on (**5**   ),
they used to keep the city streets clean. Today in Marlow, Buckinghamshire, they
are (**6**   ), majestically (**7**   ) over the rooftops. But
some are braving lower levels.

Emily Hutchinson: Something whooshed past my head.

Hurrell: Emily had stopped for a snack with her two-year-old son in Higginson Park in
Marlow.

Hutchinson: My son had a piece of his snack in each hand, and then I looked and
was like, there's nothing in that hand anymore. What's happened? And then I
(**8**   ) realised, because he was about to (**9**   ) again,
and I had to go a bit 'mamma bear' and shout and wave him away before he went,
came back for the second one.

Hurrell: The raptor left a small (**10**   ).

Hutchinson: Well I had thought it wasn't common, until I spoke, obviously straight
away, to the doctors, just thinking, well, it's a wild animal, I need to make sure
the, that he's going to be alright. Um, and they said, funnily enough, within the
last half hour we've just had another (**11**   ) of exactly the same thing
happening in exactly the same place.

Hurrell: Some (**12**   ) people leave
food out for them and it's thought that this
is encouraging these otherwise timid birds
to become more (**13**   ).

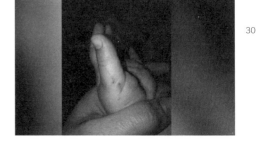

Martin Robinson, Wild Marlow: They (^{14}) naturally. There's plenty of food all the year round for them. You often see them on roadkill. Um, and, and really it's perhaps (^{15}) to their habit of actually stealing food now. So, we'd really urge people not to put food out for them.

35

40

Hurrell: Red kites are one of this country's greatest (^{16}) successes. Deliberate poisoning and egg collecting drove them to near (^{17}) in the early 20th century. Reintroduced in the late 1980s, it's thought that there are around 1,800 breeding (^{18}) in the UK today.

45

Pippa Simpson, resident: The original intentions was to breed the birds and let them (^{19}) across the UK.

Hurrell: Pippa has set up a (^{20}) to educate people as to why we shouldn't be leaving food out for them.

Simpson: By feeding them (^{21}), they're creating, um, behaviours which are not natural to the species. And they're causing the birds to (^{22}), which is then causing knock-on issues for the communities, and not just Stokenchurch, Marlow, for the Chilterns, you know, across the Chilterns there's incidences everywhere.

50

Hurrell: Over the centuries red kites have been prized and (^{23}). The future fortunes of these beautiful birds seem to depend very much on our behaviour. Wendy Hurrell, BBC London.

55

(Monday 29 June 2020)

Notes

l.3 **the Chilterns**「チルターン」ロンドン郊外、北西部にあるチルターン丘陵 (the Chiltern Hills) のこと。全長74kmで、南西から北東方向に広がっている　l.9 **William Shakespeare**「ウィリアム・シェイクスピア (1564-1616)」エリザベス朝時代 (1558-1603) を中心に活躍したイングランドを代表する劇作家　l.10 **the red kite**「アカトビ」タカ科の中型の猛禽類。主にヨーロッパに生息する。体長約60cm　l.13 **Marlow**「マーロウ」バッキンガムシャーにある町　l.13 **Buckinghamshire**「バッキンガムシャー」イングランド南東部の州　l.17 **Higginson Park**「ヒギンソン・パーク」マーロウにある公園。1758年に庭園として開園し、1926年からは公共の公園となった。面積は約9.5ヘクタールで、年間100万人が訪れている　l.22 **mamma bear**「お母さんグマ」過保護な母親を表す俗語。ここでは、なりふり構わず子供を守ろうとする母親の必死な様子を表している　l.34 **Wild Marlow**「ワイルド・マーロウ」2019年に認可された、マーロウの自然環境や生物多様性の保全のために活動するコミュニティ利益会社 (CIC: Community Interest Company)。CICとは2005年にイギリス政府によって導入された企業形態で、社会的課題の解決を目的とする組織が審査を経て認可される　l.53 **Stokenchurch**「ストークンチャーチ」バッキンガムシャー南西部の村

Unit 6 Return of the Red Kites　　35

BEHIND THE SCENES

イギリスの国鳥総選挙

　世界では国鳥が指定されている国々もありますが、イギリスでは国鳥が定められていません。そこで、鳥に関する数々の本の著者であるデイヴィッド・リンドー（David Lindo）が2015年、イギリスの国鳥を決める選挙を行いました。まずは60種類の鳥で予選を行い、その後3月から5月にかけて10種の代表から選ぶ最終選挙がオンライン、郵便投票、学校の投票箱による投票で行われました。22万4,000以上の投票が集まり、そのうち34％を占めたコマドリ（robin）が1位となりました。2位は12％のメンフクロウ（barn owl）、3位は11％のクロウタドリ（blackbird）という結果となり、ニュースで言及されたアカトビは5位でした。コマドリは人を怖がらず、庭師が土を掘ると掘り出された虫を求めてやって来るため「庭師の友達（gardener's friend）」として知られ、ビアトリクス・ポター（Beatrix Potter, 1866-1943）によるピーター・ラビット（Peter Rabbit）の絵に描かれたり、「だれがコマドリ殺したの？」（"Who Killed Cock Robin?", c. 1744）などの童謡でも歌われています。また、コマドリはクリスマス・シーズンになると、クリスマスカードやクリスマス記念切手に描かれます。コマドリはイギリスの人々にとって大変身近な存在です。

Moving On

6 Making a Summary

▶ Fill the gaps to complete the summary.

　Red kites are birds of prey, which (s   ) their food. In the days of Shakespeare, they were more than (t   ) because they kept the streets clean by eating (c   ), but by the early 20th century, they had almost become extinct, due to poisoning and egg collecting. However, they were reintroduced in the late 1980s and today there are about 1,800 breeding pairs in the UK. In Marlow, they are (u   ), but unfortunately, they sometimes (s   ) down and steal snacks from people's hands. They do this because they have become (o   ) on food (h   ), so people have been urged not to feed them. The original intention was for the birds to (d   ) across the UK, but artificial feeding has caused them to (c   ), causing issues for communities.

7 Follow Up

▶ Discuss, write or present.

1. What birds of prey are there in Japan? Are there any similar problems, with birds snatching food?

2. Why do you think that people feed these birds, even when they have been told not to? Would you give food to these birds?

3. Are there any animals or birds in Japan that are close to extinction, or have been close to extinction? Has anything been done to save them?

Unit **7**

All Cars to Be Electric

環境への配慮が注目される中、私たちのクルマ社会にも変化が求められています。自動車生産の長い歴史を誇るイギリスでは、どのような取り組みが行われているのでしょうか。

▌▌ Starting Off

1 Setting the Scene

▶ **What do you think?**

1. Do you, or your family, have a car? What makes it move: petrol, diesel, or something else?
2. Why is there a lot of concern about the fuel we use in our cars?
3. What are governments around the world doing to reduce that concern?

2 Building Language

▶ **Which word (1- 5) best fits which explanation (a-e)?**

1. forefront   [ ]   **a.** the most fundamental rule or idea
2. principle   [ ]   **b.** any substance that harms the environment, or makes it dirty
3. pollutant   [ ]   **c.** enormous, imposing; very considerable and hard to ignore
4. massive   [ ]   **d.** the distance a vehicle (or animal) is able to travel; the total products of a manufacturer or designer
5. range   [ ]   **e.** the position of most importance

3 Understanding Check 1

▶ Read the quotes, then watch the news and match them to the right people.

1. Listen to that! She sounds and she looks magnificent!   [   ]

2. I should say the report was filmed before the second lockdown ...   [   ]

3. We really do need more charge points on city streets and in towns ...   [   ]

4. ... a brand new technology, in the space of what is a few years, is an incredible challenge.   [   ]

4 Understanding Check 2

▶ Which is the best answer?

1. After what year will it be impossible to buy a new petrol or diesel car in Britain?
   a. next year
   b. 2030
   c. 2040
   d. 2050

2. What do big car companies think about the government's aim to halt sales of petrol and diesel powered cars?
   a. It is not going to be easy.
   b. They have been investing for a century, so this change should be easy.
   c. It is a good opportunity to use new technology.
   d. It will not be a problem, because they already have at least one electric car in their range.

3. The woman at the end of the video, talked about electric charge points. What important point did she not mention?
   a. They must work properly.
   b. People must know where they are, so they know they can charge their vehicles.
   c. They must not be too expensive.
   d. People without their own parking spaces must be able to use them on the streets.

4. The mechanic said that the internal combustion engine has changed everyone's lives. What examples does he give?

_____

5. According to Justin Rowlatt, the journalist, what three questions about electric vehicles still need to be answered?

_____

6. If we try driving an electric vehicle, what will we discover?

_____

BACKGROUND INFORMATION

　今回のニュースは、イギリス政府がガソリンとディーゼルを燃料とする新車の製造・販売の禁止を前倒ししたというものです。そもそもこの規制は2017年に発表され、当初ターゲットは2040年とされていましたが、ボリス・ジョンソン（Boris Johnson, 1964- ）首相がこれを2020年2月に2035年へ、次いで同年11月には2030年へと前倒すことを発表しました。この背景にあるのは、2050年までに二酸化炭素実質排出量ゼロ（net zero）、またはカーボン・ニュートラルを実現するという、国としての目標です。日本の経済産業省が2020年10月に公表した資料によると、2050年までのネットゼロを表明しているのは121ヶ国・1地域です。イギリスでは2019年夏、退陣直前の当時のテリーザ・メイ（Theresa May, 1956- ）首相が、高まる環境保護運動の声に応える形で、2050年までのネットゼロを世界に先駆けて法制化しました。このような指導的な立場を受け、イギリスは第26回国連気候変動枠組条約締約国会議（COP26）の議長国となりました。2020年にグラスゴーで会議が予定されていましたが、新型コロナウイルスの流行により1年延期が決定しました。

　この目標は現実的に実現可能なのでしょうか。ハイブリッド車については、条件付きで2035年まで新車の製造・販売が認められています。電気自動車はすでに実用化されており、充電スタンドも急速に増加しています。2015年に販売された新車のうちハイブリッドを含む電気自動車は僅か1.1%でしたが、2020年には、新車全体の需要の落ち込みはあるものの、年平均10.7%にまで伸びました。また、2020年の最初の10ヶ月間で、充電スタンドは18%増加しました。価格についても、現状では高くついてしまいますが、政府補助金と量産化により低下が見込めます。しかし、2021年3月には大手の自動車製造業者数社が政府に対し、急激すぎる規制で業界が存続の危機に瀕してしまうとして、規制内容の緩和を要望する陳述書を提出するなどしており、今後の展開に注目する必要があります。

参考：

https://www.theguardian.com/business/2021/mar/15/car-industry-lobbied-uk-government-delay-ban-petrol-diesel-cars

https://www.theguardian.com/environment/2020/oct/06/a-nine-point-plan-for-the-uk-to-achieve-net-zero-carbon-emissions

https://www.theguardian.com/environment/2020/jun/24/uks-net-zero-pledge-what-has-been-achieved-one-year-on

| News Story |

▶ **Watch the news, then fill the gaps in the text.**

Male newsreader: A (¹   ) on the sale of new petrol and diesel cars, expected to be brought forward to 2030. That is a decade earlier than (²   ) planned.

5

Female newsreader: The changes will accelerate the (³   ) towards electric vehicles, as the UK aims to reach net zero carbon emissions by 2050. Here's our chief correspondent, Justin Rowlatt. I should say the report was filmed before the second lockdown, in a Tier 1 area.

10

Justin Rowlatt: The UK has been at the (⁴   ) of the car industry since the very beginning. Designing, making, and of course, driving cars.

Rowlatt: I can't believe it, racing at Brooklands! A-ha!

Rowlatt: The car has (⁵   ) reshaped our world.

Roger Horsefield, volunteer mechanic, Brooklands: You wouldn't have the road (⁶   ) we got now: the motorways, the towns built around the, the er, the roads. Um, so, you know, the internal combustion engine really has changed everyone's lives.

15

Rowlatt: Listen to that! She sounds and she looks magnificent! But remember, the basic (⁷   ) of the internal combustion engine hasn't changed since this car was built 110 years ago. And remember, it relies on blowing up (⁸   ) gasses.

20

Rowlatt: And we know that produces carbon dioxide and other (⁹   ).

Rowlatt: Cor, it really does accelerate fast.

Rowlatt: Which is why the government isn't saying get rid of cars. Just the (¹⁰   ).

25

Rowlatt: This is the race version of Jaguar's latest electric offering, (¹¹   ) the performance of electric vehicles, even at the top end, is at least the equal of petrol.

30

Rowlatt: Most of the big car companies now have at least one electric vehicle in their (¹²   ), but they say the 2030 target is very (¹³   ).

Mike Hawes, Society of Motor Manufacturers and Traders: The challenge to the industry is absolutely (**14**   ). We've been an industry built on petrol, diesel engines for over a century. (**15**   ) that, with all the (**16**   ) investment, to a brand new technology, in the space of what is a few years, is an incredible challenge.

Rowlatt: There are still lots of questions that need to be answered. Where will we charge these electric vehicles? Will they be (**17**   )? Will they have the (**18**   ) for the journeys we need to make?

Baroness Brown, Climate Change Committee: We really do need more charge points on city streets and in towns, to (**19**   ) for the people who don't have off-street parking opportunities. They need to be around where people can see them to give them (**20**   ) they're going to be able to charge their vehicles. And they also need to work.

Rowlatt: If you've got any (**21**   ) about buying an electric car, you know what you should do? You should give one a go. Here we go.

Rowlatt: You'll find they are just as good as the fossil-fuel powered versions. And we now know where our petrol and diesel vehicles are (**22**   ). That's right. From 2030, they will be museum pieces.   *(Saturday 14 November 2020)*

> **Notes**

l.8 **net zero carbon emissions**「二酸化炭素実質排出ゼロ」二酸化炭素の人為的な排出量と、森林等が吸収することによる除去量との均衡を実現し、実質的な排出量をゼロにすること　l.10 **the second lockdown**「2度目のロックダウン」新型コロナウイルスの感染拡大を防ぐため、2020年11月5日から12月2日にかけてイギリス全土で行われた　l.10 **Tier 1**「ティア1」イギリスにおける新型コロナウイルスの警戒レベル4段階のうちの第1段階で、「中程度（Medium alert）」を表す。ティア2は「高い（High alert）」、ティア3は「非常に高い（Very High alert）」、ティア4は「自宅待機（Stay at Home）」　l.13 **Brooklands**「ブルックランズ」イングランド南東部のサリー州にあった、世界初のモーターレース専用サーキット兼飛行場。1907年に開設され、自動車レースや走行テストなどに利用されたが、1939年の第二次世界大戦の開戦に伴い閉鎖され、軍用機の製造拠点として用いられた。現在、一部はブルックランズ博物館（Brooklands Museum）となり、自動車や航空機の歴史を伝えている　l.17 **internal combustion engine**「内燃機関」ガソリンエンジンやディーゼルエンジンなどを指す　l.24 **Cor**「おっと」「おや」「えっ」イギリス英語で、驚いた時などに用いられる　l.27 **Jaguar**「ジャガー」イギリスの高級自動車メーカー。1922年設立　l.35 **Society of Motor Manufacturers and Traders**（SMMT）「自動車製造販売協会」イギリス自動車産業の業界団体。ロンドンに拠点を置き、800社以上で構成される。1902年設立　l.46 **Climate Change Committee**（CCC）「気候変動委員会」イギリスの政府外公共機関（Non-departmental public body）。「2008年気候変動法（Climate Change Act 2008）」の制定に基づき設立され、気候変動への取り組みに関して政府に助言を行っている

BEHIND THE SCENES

世界で人気の自動車番組

　BBCの『トップ・ギア』（Top Gear）は1977年に開始し、現在まで続く自動車番組です。1988年にジェレミー・クラークソン（Jeremy Clarkson, 1960-）が司会に加わった頃から人気番組となりました。現在は司会が交代したものの、過去のシリーズも含め世界各国で放送されています。クラークソンは車のレビューが辛辣なことで知られ、悪いデザインやエンジンを徹底的に酷評しました。また、大規模な車の実験も行われ、トヨタ車のハイラックスを海に沈め、鉄球をぶつけ、最後にはビルの屋上に載せてビルごと破壊した耐久テストは有名なエピソードとして知られています。番組のテストコースで有名人がラップタイムを競う企画「有名人レース（Star in a Reasonably Priced Car）」には、ヒュー・グラント（Hugh Grant, 1960-）やトム・クルーズ（Tom Cruise, 1962-）などの有名俳優だけでなく、堍首相のボリス・ジョンソンも過去に参加したことがあります。

Moving On

6 Making a Summary

 CD1-22

▶ Fill the gaps to complete the summary.

　The British government is aiming to ban the sale of new fossil-fuel powered cars after 2030. The basic (p　　　　　) of the car engine is the blowing up of (e　　　　　) gases, which produces global-warming carbon dioxide and other (p　　　　　), and so they want to accelerate the (s　　　　　) to electric vehicles. However, Britain has always been in the (f　　　　　) of the industry, and (s　　　　　) all the (e　　　　　) investment to a new technology will be a (m　　　　　) challenge. Electric vehicles must be (a　　　　　) and have sufficient (r　　　　　). Also, there must be enough (c　　　　　) points on city streets, so that drivers can be confident they can always (c　　　　　) their vehicles. There is a long way to go, but if you try an electric car now, you will find they are just as good as fossil-fuel powered versions, which by 2030 will be museum pieces.

7 Follow Up

▶ Discuss, write or present.

1　Does the Japanese government have a similar target for banning fossil-fuel powered vehicles? If so, what is it?

2　Brooklands is a famous old car-racing track that is no longer used. What do you think about car races, such as Formula 1? Are they good for the environment? Why do car companies, like Honda, invest in racing cars?

3　Are you optimistic that the British or Japanese targets will be met? Will the world be able to stop climate change? What do you think life will be like in 2050?

Mend More and Buy Less: London Repair Shops

大量に消費して大量に廃棄する使い捨て文化はイギリスの社会にも定着していますが、この問題を解決するための新たな取り組みがロンドンで行われています。一体どのようなものでしょうか。ニュースを見てみましょう。

Starting Off

1 Setting the Scene

▶ **What do you think?**

1. What do you usually do if something is broken or damaged? Do you throw it away, have somebody else repair it, or repair it yourself?
2. If you want to repair something yourself, how can you find out how to do it?
3. Think of something that you have repaired, or tried to repair, in the past few years. How did you do it? Were you successful?

2 Building Language

For each word (1-6), find two synonyms (a-l).

1. conscious   [   ][   ]
2. mend   [   ][   ]
3. sustainable   [   ][   ]
4. empowered   [   ][   ]
5. promote   [   ][   ]
6. misconception [   ][   ]

a. misunderstanding	g. repair
b. fix	h. aware
c. trained	i. advertise
d. continuous	j. mindful
e. fallacy	k. encourage
f. renewable	l. qualified

3 Understanding Check 1

▶ Read the quotes, then watch the news and match them to the right people.

1. ... but the Gen Z, um, people are coming through, and they're really being switched on ... [   ]

2. ... it's said that we live in a throw-away society, one where it's often cheaper to replace something ... [   ]

3. The London Recycles campaign has done a little bit of research ... [   ]

4. ... and find people that are already out there who can do those skills ...
[   ]

4 Understanding Check 2

▶ Which is the best answer?

1. Which of the following is correct, according to London Recycles research data?
    a. Eighty-five percent of people who repair possessions are under twenty-five.
    b. Forty-seven percent of over 55s have repaired something in the past year.
    c. Twenty-five percent of over 55s want to know how to repair something.
    d. Sixty-nine percent of Londoners are not interested in repairing anything.

2. According to the blonde woman in blue trousers, what is the most important way to encourage repairing?
    a. by making clothes more expensive, so that we want to keep them for a long time
    b. by looking after garment workers, who don't want throw-away fashion
    c. by educating people when they are young, teaching them that we shouldn't throw away clothes so often
    d. by switching on young people, and showing them that it is cool to wear repaired clothes

3. In conclusion, the reporter mentions three benefits of London Repair Week. Which one of the following does she not mention?
    a. People realise that it is much cheaper to repair things.
    b. It will teach people new skills.
    c. Repairing clothes will become more fashionable.
    d. Recycling items means that we have a more sustainable economy.

▶ **What do you remember?**

4. According to the newsreader, what is a 'throw-away' society, and how are our attitudes changing?

_____

5. What does the first shopkeeper feel is more sustainable in the long run?

_____

6. Does the last woman being interviewed (in blue trousers) think that young people in particular are just into throw-away fashion? What about Generation Z?

_____

BACKGROUND INFORMATION

　安くて手軽なファストファッションですが、大量生産と大量消費が環境にもたらす悪影響が問題となっています。イギリス庶民院の環境監査委員会（the Environmental Audit Committee）が2019年に提出した報告書によると、イギリスにおける新品の衣類の購入量は国民１人につき26.7kgで、ヨーロッパの他の国々と比べて最も多いことがわかりました。2016年にイギリスでは約113万トンの衣類が購入されましたが、一方で、年間約100万トンもの衣類が不用品として処分されています。イギリスではチャリティーが普及しているため、これらの不要となった衣類の３分の２はチャリティー・ショップへの寄付などを通じて再利用されています。しかし、なおも30万トン以上の衣類が家庭ゴミとして廃棄されており、その内の20％は埋め立て処理され、80％は焼却処分になっているのが現状です。

　ゴミの量を減らして環境に配慮した社会を実現すべく、ロンドン廃棄物・リサイクル委員会（London Waste and Recycling Board）は「ロンドン・リサイクルズ（London Recycles）」というキャンペーンを手掛けています。ホームページでは、個々の物品のリサイクルの仕方だけでなく、食品を長持ちさせる保存方法や、①新聞は紙ではなくスマートフォンで読む、②繰り返し使えるマイカップでコーヒーを飲む、③会議資料は事前にデータで配布する、といった、日々の生活の中ですぐに実践できる工夫を紹介するなどし、市民によるリサイクルを推進しています。また、活動の一環として2020年に開催された「ロンドン・リペア・ウィーク（London Repair Week）」には50を超える企業や団体が参加し、持ち物を修繕しながら末永く使うための様々な方法を提案しました。開催期間中は、ニュースでも取り上げられていた衣類をはじめとして、自転車や電化製品、家具など、多様な物品の修繕を促進するためのイベントやワークショップが行われ、修繕に興味を持つ人々が具体的な方法を知るための機会を提供しました。ちょっとした努力の積み重ねにより、やがて大きな変化が訪れることが期待されています。

参考：

https://publications.parliament.uk/pa/cm201719/cmselect/cmenvaud/1952/report-summary.html
https://londonrecycles.co.uk/
https://londonrecycles.co.uk/repair-week/

▶ Watch the news, then fill the gaps in the text.

Newsreader: Next, though, it's said that we live in a throw-away society, one where it's often cheaper to replace something than to repair it. But, our attitudes toward that changing as we become more environmentally (¹   ). Well, if the latest research is anything to go by, it appears so, with younger people leading the way when it comes to (²   ) more and buy less. Here's Wendy Hurrell.

5

Wendy Hurrell: Barley Massey has had her shop, Fabrications, on Broadway Market in Hackney for 20 years, from where she (³   ) classes. And there's increasing interest, particularly among young people, in repairing things.

10

Barley Massey, owner of Fabrications: We get so many people coming in saying, "Oh could you fix this shirt? It just needs a button (⁴   )". And we're like, "Well, no, we can't fix it for you but we can teach you", because if we feel that that's more, in the long run, (⁵   ) : that people are (⁶   ) to have those skills for themselves. You know if things aren't good enough to repair, actually you could cut it up and turn it into something new. So there's that creative, personalising, making something really unique.

15

Hurrell: The London Recycles campaign has done a little bit of research, and it turns out that 85% of people under the age of 25 have, in the last year, repaired one of their (⁷   ). And that compares to 47% of the over 55s. Sixty-nine percent of Londoners say they would repair something, if they only knew how. So, they've (⁸   ) the first London Repair Week.

20

Violetta Lynch, London Recycles: What we've really wanted to do was to show people, and teach people some really simple skills, and find people that are already out there who can do those skills, that are posting about it on social media and that have (⁹   ) and then also really (¹⁰   ) the small businesses and the shops, for those people that don't really want to do it themselves, but would love to support their local (¹¹   ), and ask their local repair shop to, to fix it for them.

25

30

Lucy Hall, co-founder of LoanHood: That's my favourite dress.

Hurrell: Lucy and Jade will have a (¹²   ) on Saturday as part of Repair Week. And they're soon (¹³   ) a clothes rental app, so even high street brands can earn their keep, while (¹⁴   ) unworn in the wardrobe.

Hurrell: Is it a (¹⁵   ) that young people in particular are into just throw-away fashion?

Hall: I think that there is some of that, (¹⁶   ). Um, but the Gen Z, um, people are coming through, and they're really being switched on about, what we want to know, like, if you're looking after your garment workers, where their items are coming from. We don't want to have this throw-away fashion. But it all comes down to education, and people are (¹⁷   ) (¹⁸   ) at a young age that these garments are really special, and that we don't have to throw them all away.

Hurrell: (¹⁹   ), and perhaps some new skills, as London Repair Week makes (²⁰   ) yet more fashionable. Wendy Hurrell, BBC London.

(Monday 12 October 2020)

Notes

l.4 **our attitudes toward that changing** 文法的に正しくは our attitudes toward that are changing となる   l.10 **Fabrications**「ファブリケーションズ」2000年6月に開店した手芸店で、スタジオや教室としても使われている   l.10 **Broadway Market**「ブロードウェイ・マーケット」ハックニーにある通り。通りを使った青空市場で知られている   l.11 **Hackney**「ハックニー」インナー・ロンドンの北東部にあるハックニーロンドン自治区を指す   l.20 **The London Recycles**「ロンドン・リサイクルズ」2007年大ロンドン庁法 (the Greater London Authority Act 2007) に基づいて設置されたロンドン廃棄物・リサイクル委員会 (London Waste and Recycling Board) が運営するキャンペーン。市民のリサイクル活動を支援している   l.24 **London Repair Week**「ロンドン・リペア・ウィーク」2020年10月12日から17日まで開催された、修繕を促進するためのイベント   l.33 **LoanHood**「ローンフッド」持続可能なファッションを目指して2019年にロンドンで設立された会社。利用者が自分の服を貸し出すことのできるアプリを2021年夏に始動する予定   l.44 **the Gen Z** (Generation Z)「ジェネレーションZ」1990年代後半から2010年代初めに生まれた世代

ファッションと手仕事の博物館

　ロンドンには博物館や美術館が数多く存在していますが、中でもサウス・ケンジントンは、主要なミュージアムの集まる地区として多くの訪問者を惹きつけています。1851年の万博の展示物を引き継ぎ、1854年にこの地に開館したサウス・ケンジントン・ミュージアム（South Kensington Museum）は、1899年にヴィクトリア・アンド・アルバート・ミュージアム（Victoria and Albert Museum）と改名しました。家具や服飾などの工芸品のコレクションは世界屈指で、洋服やアクセサリーなどファッションに関連する展示が充実しています。エリザベス1世に幽閉されたスコットランド女王メアリーが製作に関わった不死鳥のタペストリーも含まれており、王族自らの手仕事の、非常に珍しい一品となっています。

Moving On

6 Making a Summary

CD1-25

▶ Fill the gaps to complete the summary.

　Our attitudes to the (t　　　　　) society are changing as we become more environmentally (c　　　　　). And young people in particular are becoming more likely to (m　　　　) more and buy less. While only 47% of over 55s have repaired a possession in the past year, 85% of the under 25s have done so. This shop, called Fabrications, doesn't fix things for customers, but teaches them how to repair things for themselves, as it is more (s　　　　　) if people are (e　　　　　) to have those skills. There is also a (s　　　　　), and local shops that will repair things are (p　　　　　). Gen Z people are more switched on, and aware of how their garments are made, and where they come from, so it is a (m　　　　　) to think that young people are just into (t　　　　　) fashion. London Repair Week is aiming at (s　　　　) and making (m　　　　　) more fashionable.

7 Follow Up

▶ Discuss, write or present.

1. Do you agree that young people are more likely to repair things than older people? Or does the data surprise you? Why do you think under 25s might be more likely to have repaired something recently?

2. What does the 'throw-away society' mean? This story just talks about clothes, but can you think of other examples? Are there industries that are more wasteful than the fashion industry, and what can be done about it?

3. Do you agree that "it all comes down to education"? Should schools have a role in developing a more sustainable economy?

Unit 9

Swimming to Cure Dementia

少子高齢化が進行しつつある現在、老後の健康への関心が高まっています。寒中水泳がもたらす健康への効能について、ニュースを見てみましょう。

Starting Off

1 Setting the Scene

▶ What do you think?

1. How do you feel about swimming? Are you a good swimmer? Where and how often do you go swimming?

2. What do you think of those people who go swimming outside in the winter? Have you ever done it?

3. What do you know about dementia? Do you know of someone with dementia? Can it be cured or prevented?

2 Building Language

▶ Which word (1-6) best fits which explanation (a-f)?

1. exposure   [   ]   **a.** start something or cause a change
2. trigger   [   ]   **b.** a group of people with something in common
3. degenerative [   ]   **c.** existing without people noticing; not obvious
4. latent   [   ]   **d.** being in a place with no protection against something
5. chilly   [   ]   **e.** steadily becomes worse over time
6. cohort   [   ]   **f.** a bit cold

Watching the News

3 Understanding Check 1

▶ Read the quotes, then watch the news and match them to the right people.

1. Which is where this place, Hampstead Heath Lido, comes in. [   ]

2. ... that would have an enormous impact economically and healthwise. [   ]

3. Research by scientists at Cambridge University suggests that ... [   ]

4. Well, we're from the North so we can handle it. [   ]

4 Understanding Check 2

▶ Which is the best answer?

1. What are the scientists investigating?
   a. They want to know why people enjoy swimming in cold water.
   b. They are looking for a protein that can protect us from the cold.
   c. They are trying to find out whether humans can hibernate like animals.
   d. They are looking for something that might delay dementia.

2. What happens when animals hibernate?
   a. Their brain cells are reformed while they sleep.
   b. Their brain cells miraculously grow.
   c. They lose some connections between brain cells, which are reformed when they wake up.
   d. While they are sleeping, their brains are protected by a protein.

3. Why were the scientists interested in people who regularly get very cold?
   a. They wanted to see if the cold induces the production of a protective protein.
   b. Cold people are miraculously reformed in the spring, like animals.
   c. They wanted to see whether cold swimming gives better protection than tai chi.
   d. Some people seem to hibernate when they are cold, and this might cure dementia.

4. Why were those people gathering at Hampstead Heath Lido?

_____

5. Why must we be careful if we go swimming in winter?

_____

6. If we could slow dementia by a couple of years, what impact would it have?

_____

BACKGROUND INFORMATION

　国民保健サービス（NHS: National Health Service）によれば、イギリスでは現在85万人以上が認知症を患っており、65歳以上の14人に1人、80歳以上では6人に1人の数に上ります。2025年には、認知症の患者数が100万人以上まで増加すると予測されています。

　世界の認知症研究をリードするべく、イギリスでは2015年2月、当時のデイヴィッド・キャメロン首相（David Cameron, 1966- ）が「2020年認知症に対する行動計画（the Prime Minister's Challenge on Dementia 2020）」を発表し、2020年までにイギリスが認知症のケアと支援において世界最高の国となること、認知症およびその他の神経退行性疾患の研究において世界最高の場所となることを目標としました。その計画では、認知症に関する理解、早期診断、適切なケアなどの促進とともに、2025年までに認知症の正しい治療法を明らかにする目標が掲げられています。行動計画には国際的な認知症の研究施設を作るという目標も立てられ、2017年、イギリス認知症研究所（UK DRI: UK Dementia Research Institute）が設立されました。ロンドンに本部があり、ユニバーシティ・カレッジ・ロンドン（University College London）などの6つの大学にあるそれぞれのセンターで、600人以上の研究者が認知症に関する世界的研究を行っています。

　2015年、ジョヴァンナ・マルッチ（Giovanna Mallucci）教授のチームは、科学誌『ネイチャー』（Nature）にて、退行性疾患の発症を遅らせるRBM3という低温ショックタンパク質（cold-shock protein）が低体温になったマウスから検出されたことを発表しました。しかし、人体におけるRBM3の役割に関する実験については、倫理的な問題で人を低体温状態にする許可を取るのが難しいとマルッチ教授はBBCラジオ4の『トゥデイ』（Today）で話しました。それに対し、屋外プールで冬も泳いでいるスイマーのグループが協力を申し出て、2016年から3年間、彼らの血中におけるRBM3の濃度を調べることになりました。今後、この最先端の研究に基づいて、認知症の発症を遅らせる方法を見つけることが期待されています。

参考：

https://ukdri.ac.uk/
https://www.gov.uk/government/publications/prime-ministers-challenge-on-dementia-2020
https://www.bbc.com/news/health-54531075

5 Filling Gaps | News Story | ○CD2-02 [Original] ○CD2-03 [Voiced]

▶ Watch the news, then fill the gaps in the text.

Newsreader: Could swimming in cold water be linked to a possible cure for dementia? Research by scientists at Cambridge University suggests that (**1**   ) to the cold can (**2**   ) the production of a protein that may protect the brain from (**3**   )

diseases. Our chief environment correspondent, Justin Rowlatt, a (**4**   ) cold water swimmer himself, explains.

Justin Rowlatt: Fancy a dip? Yes, in cold water.

First swimmer: No, it's warm, it's warm, yeah. Ah!

Second swimmer: Well, we're from the North so we can handle it. Ha, ha, ha.

Rowlatt: So why might this help protect against dementia?

Rowlatt: The answer is a (**5**   ) hibernation ability prompted by getting cold that it seems human beings (**6**   ).

Rowlatt: When animals hibernate, they (**7**   ) some of the connections between their brain cells. But they are miraculously (**8**   ) when they wake in the spring, thanks in part to a protein discovered by the Cambridge University team.

Rowlatt: Which is where this place, Hampstead Heath Lido, comes in.

Rowlatt: The scientists wanted to know if our bodies produce the same protein, and needed a group of people who (**9**   ) get very cold.

Professor Giovanna Mallucci, UK Dementia Research Institute, University of Cambridge: Heat isn't probably as good for you as cold in that way ...

Rowlatt: After three years of winter blood tests, the (**10**   ) of the trial are gathered beside the (**11**   ) pool to hear the results of Professor Mallucci's work.

Mallucci: We've (**12**   ) you to a bunch of people doing tai chi, who didn't get cold. And none of them get increased (**13**   ) of this protein but, but many of you did. So what does it tell us? It tells us that cold does (**14**   ) this protein in humans. You are the first,

sort of, non-patient (¹⁵   ) to
show that cold water swimming raises this
protective protein, which is pretty cool.

Rowlatt: But remember, winter swimming can
be really dangerous if you're not used to it,
or have an (¹⁶   ) illness. So
do be careful.

Rowlatt: The challenge now is to find a drug that (¹⁷   ) the
production of the protein in humans, and, of course, to prove it really does help
(¹⁸   ) dementia.

Mallucci: If you slowed the (¹⁹   ) of dementia by even a couple of years
on a whole population, that would have an enormous impact economically and
healthwise.

Rowlatt: The link between cold water and dementia is a very (²⁰   ) line of
research, but don't expect results soon. There is, the scientists say, lots more work
to be done before it (²¹   ) a potential treatment. Justin Rowlatt, BBC
News, London.

(Monday 19 October 2020)

Notes

l.20 **Hampstead Heath Lido** 「ハムステッド・ヒース屋外プール」ロンドン北部ハムステッド・ヒース
のパーラメント・ヒルにある屋外プール。正式名称 Parliament Hill Lido。1938年設立　l.23 **UK
Dementia Research Institute**「イギリス認知症研究所」ケンブリッジ大学内の研究機関。2017年設立

BEHIND THE SCENES

ドーバー海峡を泳いで渡った男

　イギリスとフランスを隔てるドーバー海峡（the Strait of Dover）は直線距離にして約34kmという狭い海峡で、これまで数多の挑戦者たちが様々な方法による横断を試みてきました。記録に残る中では、1785年に気球を用いた初の横断が、1816年には外輪式蒸気船による渡航が成し遂げられていますが、1875年、ついに自分の体ひとつで海の向こう側に辿りつく人物が現れます。8月24日午後12時56分、イギリス人のマシュー・ウェッブ（Matthew Webb, 1848-83）はケント州の町ドーバーを平泳ぎで出発し、潮流に幾度となく行く手を阻まれつつも、翌25日午前10時41分、フランスのカレー（Calais）に無事上陸しました。21時間45分に及んだウェッブの挑戦は、人為的な助けを借りずにドーバー海峡を遠泳横断した世界初の記録となりました。一躍時の人となったウェッブでしたが、1883年、ナイアガラ川の急流を泳ごうとして失敗し、35歳という若さでこの世を去りました。

Moving On

6 Making a Summary

▶ Fill the gaps to complete the summary.

　　Dementia is a serious (d　　　　　) disease, and a delay in its progress would have an (i　　　　　) not only on our health, but also our economy. Scientists have discovered that when animals hibernate in the cold, they lose some connections between brain cells, but these are reformed when they wake up, thanks to a special protein. Humans also have a (l　　　　　) hibernating ability, and a professor is testing them to find out if (e　　　　　) to the cold will (t　　　　　) the production of the same protein. A bunch of swimmers in a (c　　　　　) pool have been tested for three years, and now they are waiting for the results. The professor found that they were the first (c　　　　　) to show that cold water swimming does raise the level of this protein. So now they need to find a drug that can (s　　　　　) its production without needing to get cold.

7 Follow Up

▶ Discuss, write or present.

1. Would you be willing to take part in research like this?
2. The reporter said that swimming in cold water is dangerous if you are not used to it, but do you know why it is dangerous?
3. It is important to find a cure for dementia. But are there other diseases for which we need to find cures? Are there any that are more important than dementia? For example, is it important that we find a cure for Covid-19?

Unit 10

A Special Pop-up Shop on Carnaby Street

人種差別の撤廃が声高に叫ばれる中、流行の発信地ロンドンのショッピングストリートに、他とは違うファッションの店が出現しました。一体どのような背景があるのでしょうか。ニュースを見てみましょう。

Starting Off

1 Setting the Scene

▶ **What do you think?**

1. Are you interested in fashion? What kind of clothes do you like to buy?
2. Where do you buy your clothes? Do you care who they are made by?
3. What sort of clothes are in fashion at the moment?

2 Building Language

▶ **Which word (1-6) best fits which explanation (a-f)?**

1. showcase   [   ]   **a.** most expensive or sophisticated
2. entrepreneur [   ]   **b.** display something in a place that makes it look good
3. struggle   [   ]   **c.** relating to someone's personal tastes and emotions
4. subjective   [   ]   **d.** have difficulty in doing something
5. engage   [   ]   **e.** take part in something, or become involved
6. high-end   [   ]   **f.** a businessperson that invests for profit

3 Understanding Check 1

▸ Read the quotes, then watch the news and match them to the right people.

1. Visibility is everything. [ ]
2. But a new shop has opened up today with a difference. [ ]
3. And, as the saying goes, we are all one ... [ ]
4. So, there's definitely those buyers who've been ahead of the curve. [ ]

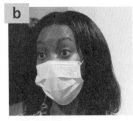

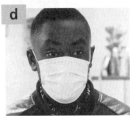

4 Understanding Check 2

▸ Which is the best answer?

1. What is special about this new shop in Carnaby Street?
   a. It sells clothes specially made for black people.
   b. The businesses in the shop are all owned by black people.
   c. Only black people are working there.
   d. All the customers are people of colour.

2. Why did the shop owners choose Carnaby Street?
   a. Other black-owned businesses are very visible in Carnaby Street.
   b. They can connect with people they probably wouldn't be able to meet elsewhere.
   c. Lots of black people who live near Carnaby Street are very visible.
   d. Their businesses can succeed because they can share the same bubble.

3. What is the most important thing for Koby Martin, the artist?
   a. The businesses will be able to succeed at last.
   b. Being an entrepreneur is an amazing feeling.
   c. Different races are able to meet each other as equals.
   d. The art being created is very subjective.

▶ **What do you remember?**

4. When and why was Carnaby Street most famous?

---

5. What was the first person, a fashion designer, selling, and what was she hoping for?

---

6. How long will the shop be there, and what is hoped will happen next?

BACKGROUND INFORMATION

　カーナビー・ストリートは、ロンドンの繁華街ソーホーの中心にあります。高級店が立ち並ぶリージェント・ストリートと並走するこの歩行者天国の商店街は、ポップな若者の文化を象徴しています。スウィンギング・シックスティーズと言われた1960年代には、ジミ・ヘンドリックス（Jimi Hendrix, 1942-70）、ビートルズ（The Beatles）、ローリング・ストーンズ（The Rolling Stones）らのロックスターや、女優エリザベス・テイラー（Elizabeth Taylor, 1932-2011）らのファッションリーダーが集い、ベジタリアンレストランやファッションブティックが軒を並べました。1970年代には、セックス・ピストルズ（The Sex Pistols）の有名な写真とともに、パンクブームがこの通りを席捲しました。1980年代にはヴィヴィアン・ウェストウッド（Vivian Westwood）ら新進気鋭のUKデザイナーが進出し、2000年代にはヒップホップの中心地となりました。2012年にはローリング・ストーンズ結成50周年を祝い、また、2018年には映画『ボヘミアン・ラプソディー』（Bohemian Rhapsody）のリリースを記念して、ロックグループ、クイーン（Queen）のイルミネーションが設置されました。

　2020年5月25日、アメリカのミネアポリスで、アフリカ系アメリカ人のジョージ・フロイド（George Floyd, 1973-2020）が4人の白人警官に拘束され、死亡するという事件が起きました。この出来事をきっかけにブラック・ライブズ・マター（BLM: Black Lives Matter）運動が起き、全米、そして世界中に広がりました。イギリスでは、1987年以来毎年10月を「黒人歴史月間（Black History Month）」として、黒人の歴史や文化、偉人の功績などを称えていますが、2020年は人種差別撤廃に向けて世論が大きく動きました。そして、今まで日の目を見てこなかった黒人による文化に光を当てる試みが実行されました。その流れを受けて、2020年10月、流行の中心地であるカーナビー・ストリートに「マイ・ランウェイ・グループ（My Runway Group）」の主催する「#ブラック・イン・カーナビー（#BlackInCarnaby）」というテーマの店舗が出現しました。黒人が経営する50以上の企業が出店し、ファッション、美容、アート、文学、映画、写真などの分野のブランドやクリエイターが、優れた製品や作品を披露しました。店舗は期間限定ですが、現代のイギリスを正しく反映するビジネスモデルを、恒久的に築く努力が続いています。

参考：
https://www.carnaby.co.uk/history/
https://www.blackhistorymonth.org.uk/section/news-views/
https://www.bbc.co.uk/newsround/49883230

5 Filling Gaps | News Story | CD2-05 [Original] CD2-06 [Voiced]

▶ Watch the news, then fill the gaps in the text.

Newsreader: Carnaby Street, the fashion (¹) in central London is probably best known for its time in the swinging sixties. But a new shop has opened up today with a difference. It'll (²) the best goods on offer

5

from black-owned businesses. Ayshea Buksh has more.

Ayshea Buksh: It's a street with a long history of fashion and style in the (³) of London's West End. And for the first time, a group of black (⁴) have been given shop space for free on Carnaby Street. 10

Buksh: Fashion designer Ade Hassan has been selling lingerie in different skin (⁵) for over six years but has (⁶) to sell her idea to major West End retailers.

Ade Hassan, Nubian Skin: Just showing that black brands can be (⁷) and do deserve to be in, you know, spaces like Carnaby Street, Regent Street. So, 15 there's definitely those buyers who've been ahead of the curve. Um, but by and large, I think a lot of the major retailers have not been. Um, and the ones that have been are, are few and far between.

Buksh: The man behind the idea hopes black businesses such as these will have a (⁸) on our high streets well beyond Black History Month. 20

Kojo Marfo, My Runway Group: Visibility is everything. The reason why we've (⁹) Carnaby, the reason why we're here is to make sure that a lot of black-owned businesses get the visibility that they, um, they (¹⁰) and that they need as well. And then also, it also introduces them to new audiences and ones that they probably might not find, er, find online or 25 (¹¹) with, and sometimes you'd think that you're doing very well online as a business, but you're all sharing the same bubble or (¹²) of audience. However, when you come out to the (¹³) world, when

you're in a place like Carnaby Street, you meet people that you'll probably will never see, or connect with, or the internet can give you.

30

Buksh: And artist Koby Martin says he believes the mix of different people here is (¹⁴) making a difference.

35

58

Koby Martin, artist: People walk in, and, take in your work, you know. And as an artist, you, you're (¹⁵   ) from your point of view, but art is very (¹⁶   ). And the most important thing for me as an artist is to connect, with people, from all (¹⁷   ). And, as

the saying goes, we are all one, you know. And, and we are all (¹⁸   ). And to, to have this My Runway Group do this for, for each and every one of us is, is such an (¹⁹   ) feeling.

Buksh: The (²⁰   ) shop will be here until the end of the year and then it's hoped other towns and cities will also (²¹   ) black excellence on their high streets. Ayshea Buksh, BBC London, Carnaby Street.

(Friday 9 October 2020)

Notes

l.1 **Carnaby Street**「カーナビー・ストリート」ロンドン中心部、シティ・オブ・ウェストミンスターのソーホー地区にある通り　l.3 **the swinging sixties**「スウィンギング・シックスティーズ」ロンドンを発信地として、ファッションや音楽、アートにおける若者中心のポップカルチャーが世界的に大流行した時代。デザイナーのマリー・クヮント（Mary Quant, 1930- ）が手掛けたミニスカートが大人気となり、ロックバンドのビートルズ（The Beatles）が台頭した時代として知られる　l.9 **West End**「ウェスト・エンド」ロンドン中心部にある地区。多くの娯楽施設や商業施設がある　l.14 **Nubian Skin**「ヌビアン・スキン」アデ・ハッサン（1984- ）が2014年に創業した、有色人種の女性向けの肌着などを扱うブランド。ロンドンに拠点を持つ　l.15 **Regent Street**「リージェント・ストリート」ウェスト・エンドにある有名なショッピングストリート　l.20 **Black History Month**「黒人歴史月間」黒人の歴史や文化、偉人の功績などを称える年中行事。1926年にアメリカで行われた「ニグロ歴史週間（Negro History Week）」を前身とし、1970年代からは期間が1ヶ月に拡大され、毎年2月に行われるようになった。「アフリカ系アメリカ人歴史月間（African-American History Month）」とも呼ばれる。イギリスでは1987年に始まって以来、毎年10月に行われている　l.21 **My Runway Group**「マイ・ランウェイ・グループ」若手の黒人クリエイターを支援する活動を行っている組織。2013年にコジョ・マルフォによって設立された　l.27 **bubble**「バブル」bubbleには「泡」「シャボン玉」という意味の他に、家族や友人や同僚など一定の人々のみで構成された「グループ」という意味があり、感染症の拡大を防ぐために外部との接触を避ける場合などに用いられる。ここでは、2020年の新型コロナウイルスの流行下において、感染拡大のリスクを最小限に留めるべく推進された「ソーシャル・バブル（social bubble）」を指している　l.31 **the internet can give you** 正しくは the internet can never give you となる　l.47 **black excellence**「ブラック・エクセレンス」優秀な能力を持つ黒人や、そうした黒人による偉業を表す。アメリカで1950年代から60年代にかけて行われたアフリカ系アメリカ人公民権運動（African-American Civil Rights Movement）から生まれた言葉

ウェッジウッドと奴隷制廃止運動

　イギリス最大の陶器メーカーであるウェッジウッド社は1759年、ジョサイア・ウェッジウッド (Josiah Wedgwood, 1730-1795) によって設立されました。王室御用達の陶工として有名であったウェッジウッドは、トマス・クラークソン (Thomas Clarkson, 1760-1846) らの奴隷制廃止論者に賛同し、1787年に組織された奴隷貿易廃止協会 (the Society for the Abolition of the Slave Trade) のために自らの資金でメダルを作成し、配布しました。メダルには手を鎖につながれて跪く黒人奴隷の姿とともに「私は人でも同胞でもないのか？ (AM I NOT A MAN AND A BROTHER?)」と記されています。大量に作られたこのメダルは、奴隷制度廃止を支持する人々のファッションアイテムとなり、嗅ぎ煙草入れの蓋、靴の留め金、ヘアピン、ペンダント、ブレスレットなどに使用されました。メダルは奴隷貿易廃止運動のエンブレムとなり、その結果イギリスでは1807年に奴隷貿易が廃止されました。

Moving On

6 Making a Summary

CD2-07

▶ Fill the gaps to complete the summary.

　Carnaby Street is a London fashion centre, most famous in the swinging sixties but still important. A group of black (e　　　　　　) have been given some free shop space there so that they can (s　　　　) their goods until the end of the year. One designer said she had (s　　　　) to sell her idea of skin tone lingerie to West End (r　　　　), but in Carnaby Street, she has the opportunity to show them that black brands can be (h　　　　). One of the (e　　　　　) said that (v　　　　) was everything: they are introduced to new audiences that they might not be able to (e　　　　) with online. But business is not everything. One artist pointed out that art was (s　　　　), and the important thing was for people of all races to connect as equals. Next year, it is hoped that black excellence will also be (s　　　　) in other towns and cities.

7 Follow Up

▶ Discuss, write or present.

1. What do you think of this idea to help black businesses? Is there anything at all like it in Japan?

2. Look on the web for some descriptions and videos of Carnaby Street in the sixties and today. Is there anywhere similar in Japan?

3. Do you agree with the artist that the most important thing is for people of all races to be able to connect as equals?

Unit 11

School Laptops for All

パンデミックで全国の学校が休校を余儀無くされ、オンライン授業が普及する中、情報格差が浮き彫りとなりました。この問題にイギリスはどのような対処をしたのでしょうか。ニュースを見てみましょう。

Starting Off

1 Setting the Scene

▶ **What do you think?**

1. Do you have a laptop computer that you can use any time you like?
2. If you have a laptop, what do you use it for? (Or if you don't have one, what would you use it for?)
3. Do you think that laptops are important for education? If so, in what way?

2 Building Language

▶ **Which word (1-7) best fits which explanation (a-g)?**

1. adequate   [   ]   **a.** put somebody into danger or an embarrassing position
2. scramble   [   ]   **b.** as good or as much as is necessary for a purpose, and no more
3. adapt   [   ]   **c.** solve or deal with a problem
4. compromise   [   ]   **d.** change or adjust because the situation has changed
5. structure   [   ]   **e.** organisation or planning
6. impact   [   ]   **f.** strong influence or effect
7. address   [   ]   **g.** move hurriedly to achieve a goal, usually in a disorderly way

3 Understanding Check 1

▶ Read the quotes, then watch the news and match them to the right people.

1. ... the most disadvantaged children, even after schools return.   [   ]

2. I do worry, especially where the world of work is going now.   [   ]

3. I found it hard to work, as, er, my little brother and I had to share the computer to work.   [   ]

4. So now we do all classes, so we are improving with the laptop.   [   ]

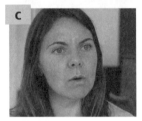 

4 Understanding Check 2

▶ Which is the best answer?

1. What issue has the BBC radio *Make a Difference* campaign been highlighting?
   a. Schools are using too much online learning.
   b. Some school pupils don't have access to adequate technology.
   c. We need to find the key to improving life's chances.
   d. Schoolchildren don't know how to use computers.

2. Which of the following advantages of having a laptop was <u>not</u> mentioned?
   a. The screen is big enough to be able to see all the homework.
   b. It gives the pupils more structure.
   c. The children don't have to share the computer.
   d. They are able to access a lot of information.

3. Which of the following sentences is correct?
   a. The government has spent 200,000 pounds on new laptops for children.
   b. The government has given laptops to over a million children who are learning at home.
   c. The government has spent 100 million pounds to help children learn at home.
   d. Havering Council has distributed laptops to every child in London who needs one.

4. How has the food bank near Wembley been helping?

_____

5. According to the man in the food bank, how do you get people out of poverty?

_____

6. Fifteen-year-old Raphy got his laptop through school, but how did his school provide laptops?

_____

BACKGROUND INFORMATION

　イギリスにおける新型コロナウイルスによる総死者数が100名を超え、1日の感染者数が2,626人に増加した2020年3月18日、イギリス政府は国内の全ての学校を同月20日から閉鎖することを発表しました。新型コロナウイルスの影響でヨーロッパの国々が続々と学校の閉鎖を発表する中、国内での対応が待たれていた状況での発表となりましたが、学校はオンライン授業の準備や宿題の作成といった対応に追われることになりました。

　エッセンシャル・ワーカーの子供やケアが必要な生徒以外はオンライン授業を受けることになりましたが、オンライン授業を受けるためのパソコンやインターネット接続が無い子供たちがいることが問題となりました。当初は180万人の子供が家にパソコンが無い状態であったと推定されています。それに対し、教育省（DfE: Department for Education）は4月、必要な機材やインターネット接続のない生徒たちにノートパソコン、タブレット、4Gのルーターなどを配布することを発表し、5月から7月の間に20万台のノートパソコンとワイヤレスルーターが配布されました。

　政府の支援だけに留まらず、困っている子供たちを手助けしようとする様々な動きが民間でも出てきました。『違いを作ろう』（_Make a Difference_）キャンペーンは2020年3月、BBCローカルラジオの全39局によって開始され、ロックダウン中に地元の人たちで意見を交換し、助け合うことを目的としています。その一環として、パソコンが無くて困っている生徒たちを助けようとする試みがなされました。個人からの寄付で4万6,000台、企業からの提供で7万台のノートパソコンが集められ、さらに約92万ポンド（約1億4,000万円）の寄付が集まり、学校や個人などに贈られました。

　イギリス財政研究所（IFS: The Institute for Fiscal Studies）が2020年に実施した4歳から15歳までの子供を持つ4,000人以上の親を対象とするオンライン授業に関する調査によれば、裕福な家庭の子供のほうが収入が少ない家庭の子供に比べて30%勉強に多くの時間を使い、収入が少ない家庭の子供の58%が自分の勉強スペースを持っていないとの結果が出ました。学校の閉鎖とオンライン授業により、教育格差がさらに広がってしまったことが判明し、今後の対策が求められます。

参考：
https://www.gov.uk/government/news/schools-colleges-and-early-years-settings-to-close
https://www.bbc.co.uk/programmes/articles/5SqHJMTKZx5sYhlltXJvB1Q/give-a-laptop

5 Filling Gaps | News Story

⊙ CD2-08 [Original] ⊙ CD2-09 [Voiced]

▶ **Watch the news, then fill the gaps in the text.**

Newsreader: We know how important online learning has been during this (¹   ), so it's important to have access to (²   ) technology, with some saying it's key to improving life's chances. As we've been hearing, BBC local radio's *Make a Difference* campaign has been highlighting the issue. Tolu Adeoye has been speaking to some of those (³   ) in London, who've received help and support.

Tolu Adeoye: It's a (⁴   ) that's been highlighted since schools closed to most children in March. Those with good access to technology and internet at home, those without.

Raphy: I found it hard to work, as, er, my little brother and I had to share the computer to work.

Sara: We used to use our phones, which was a little bit of work, a small screen which was difficult because half of the homework was not shown on there, and we used to get in trouble for not doing the (⁵   ).

Adeoye: Charities have been (⁶   ) to help. This food bank near Wembley has (⁷   ) to the need by fundraising for laptops.

Aseem Mulji, Founding Trustee, Sufra NW London: In order to get people out of poverty, and you know, (⁸   ) and generational poverty trap that they're into, you have to give people life chances, and having no digital access really (⁹   ) them for the future.

Adeoye: Sisters Sara and Heba are among those who've been helped by the charity. They're relieved not to be (¹⁰   ) on their mobiles.

Heba: The best thing about the laptop is, um, it, it's a big screen, you can do work more better in it.

Sara: So now we do all classes, so we are improving with the laptop.

Adeoye: In Tufnell Park, 15-year-old Raphy, who was (¹¹   ) an old computer with his brother, got his own laptop through school.

5

10

15

20

25

30

Raphy: I feel like it gives me, er, more
(12   ), having a laptop, I wake
up, I turn the laptop on. I've got lessons
that I don't have to think about what time
I'm doing it. Hundred per cent way better.

Adeoye: His   school   has   largely
(13   ) laptops through private
donations and fundraising.

Adeoye: Do you worry about the future for kids, particularly kids in state schools, when
it comes to the (14   ) (15   ) and catching up?

Martha Collins, Deputy Headteacher: I do worry, especially where the world of work
is going now. Er, Covid-19 means that, er, we're not going back to the way we were.
Preparing young people for that, er, is, is very different.

Adeoye: The government says it has (16   ) over 100 million pounds to
support children to learn at home, including (17   ) of over 200,000
laptops and tablets, for the children who need them most. These laptops, which are
being (18   ) by Havering Council, are some of them. But there are
still children waiting across London.

Adeoye: The worry is, unless even more is done to (19   ) that, the digital
divide will continue to (20   ) the most disadvantaged children, even
after schools return. Tolu Adeoye, BBC London.

(Wednesday 8 July 2020)

Notes

l.18 **food bank**「フードバンク」寄付された食料を貯蔵し、生活に困っている人に分配する活動および団体
l.18 **Wembley**「ウェンブリー」グレイター・ロンドン北西部のブレント区にある地域。国設スポーツ競技
場が有名　l.20 **Sufra NW London**「スフラ・ノースウェスト・ロンドン」ロンドンのブレント区に2013
年に設立された地域慈善団体　l.31 **Tufnell Park**「タフネル・パーク」グレイター・ロンドン北部のイズ
リントン区にある地域　l.50 **Havering**「ヘイバリング」グレイター・ロンドン北東部の区

BEHIND THE SCENES

コンピュータを表す英語

　日本語の「パソコン」とはpersonal computerの略称で、初期の大型で高価なコンピュータと異なり、個人で購入し使うことのできる情報処理装置として1970年代にアメリカで登場しました。パソコンの一種であるデスクトップ・コンピュータは、英語でもdesktop computerと呼ばれ、その名の通り、卓上に設置して使われます。一方、「ノートパソコン」は、英語ではlaptop computerという名称が一般的です。軽量で持ち運びが可能であり、膝（lap）の上でも使用できることからそう呼ばれるようになりました。また、小型の携帯機器である「タブレット（tablet）」の語源は「小さなテーブル」を意味する古フランス語tabletで、英語では書き物をするための「平らな石板」の意味で14世紀から使われるようになりました。ちなみにアップル（Apple）社のタブレット製品であるiPadのpadとは、メモ帳やスケッチブックなど、綴じられた用紙の束を意味する英語です。

Moving On　　6 Making a Summary　

▶ **Fill the gaps to complete the summary.**

　　Online learning has been very important, so children need to have access to (a   ) technology. There is a divide between those with good access to the internet at home, and those without. Some children have to share computers, or use their phones. Having such limited digital access really (c   ) them for the future, and so charities have been (s   ) to help. One food bank near Wembley has (a   ) to the need by fundraising for laptops. Two sisters who have been helped are relieved not to be relying on mobiles, and can work better on the big screen. One school has provided laptops through donations and fundraising and a pupil says that having one is much better because it gives him (s   ). The government has provided over 100 million pounds, and delivered over 200,000 laptops and tablets, but children are still waiting. If we don't (a   ) the issue, the digital divide will continue to (i   ) the most disadvantaged children.

7 Follow Up

▶ **Discuss, write or present.**

1. Do you agree that the government should spend money on providing laptops to children? Can you see any problems in this approach? Are there better ways that those children could be helped?

2. During the pandemic in Japan, have a lot of children and students been learning online? Does the same 'digital divide' exist, with some people not having adequate access to technology? If so, what has been done about it?

3. Raphy, who got his own laptop, said that it gave him structure, and described what he meant. Does your day have structure like that? Do you think it is important to have structure?

A New Nuclear Power Station

近年、地球環境に優しいエネルギーの供給が求められていますが、イギリスにおける原子力発電は今後どのような道を辿るのでしょうか。ニュースを見てみましょう。

Starting Off

1 Setting the Scene

▶ **What do you think?**

1. What are the various ways in which a country's electricity can be generated?
2. What do you know about nuclear power stations?
3. Why do you think a country would want to build a nuclear power station? Do you think these are good reasons?

2 Building Language

▶ **For each word (1-7), find two synonyms (a-n).**

1. replication	[ ][ ]	**a.** shut down	**h.** deactivate
2. formidable	[ ][ ]	**b.** imitation	**i.** daunting
3. colossal	[ ][ ]	**c.** persuasive	**j.** enormous
4. blunt	[ ][ ]	**d.** unsophisticated	**k.** rough
5. crude	[ ][ ]	**e.** intimidating	**l.** huge
6. compelling	[ ][ ]	**f.** direct	**m.** copy
7. decommission	[ ][ ]	**g.** irresistible	**n.** straightforward

3 Understanding Check 1

▶ Read the quotes, then watch the news and match them to the right people.

1. There are cheaper ways of making electricity, and arguably there are greener ways ...   [   ]
2. So, nuclear design takes a long time to get approved for each individual country ...   [   ]
3. Nobody thinks that nuclear is going to solve all the problems ...   [   ]
4. ... and have told the BBC they remain committed to new nuclear in order to hit that target.   [   ]

a

b

c

d

4 Understanding Check 2

▶ Which is the best answer?

1. Which one of the following sentences is correct?
   a. Currently, around 80% of the UK's electricity supply is not generated by nuclear energy.
   b. Six plants have been built, but three of them have collapsed.
   c. At the moment, the only plant under construction in the UK is Sizewell in Suffolk.
   d. Only one of the UK's nuclear plants is due to be decommissioned by 2030.

2. Which of the following sentences is correct?
   a. Hinkley will be built in 20 years and will cost more than 10 billion pounds.
   b. Sizewell will cost nearly 20 billion pounds, and construction will take about 10 years.
   c. The construction of Sizewell will take about 10 years, and cost more than 20 billion pounds.
   d. Hinkley will take ten years to build, and cost the best part of 20 billion pounds.

3. Which of the following sentences about wind farms is not correct?
   a. The price of electricity produced by the turbines today is 70% below what it was ten years ago.
   b. The area of one of the blades is greater than a football pitch.
   c. The government wants to put a turbine in every home.
   d. The tips of the blades move through the air at a speed of more than 200 mph.

▶ **What do you remember?**

4. What is the connection between Hinkley and Sizewell C?

_____

5. According to energy experts, why is it difficult to make comparisons between wind farms and nuclear power stations?

_____

6. Why does it look as if the government will approve the construction of the Sizewell C nuclear power station?

_____

■ BACKGROUND INFORMATION ■

　イギリスは2050年までに二酸化炭素実質排出量ゼロ（net zero）を実現することを目指し、脱炭素化の動きを進めています。地球温暖化対策やエネルギーの安定供給という観点から、政府は原子力発電を重視する方針でしたが、一方、再生可能エネルギーである風力発電の技術向上とコスト低下も近年目覚ましいものとなっています。2020年のイギリスにおけるエネルギー供給の内訳は、天然ガス34.5％、風力24.8％、原子力17.2％、輸入電力8.4％、バイオマス6.5％、太陽光4.4％、水力1.6％、石炭1.6％、蓄電0.5％で、風力発電が原子力発電を大きく上回るようになりました。

　一般に原子炉の寿命は40年前後とされており、電力供給を維持するためには古い原子炉の廃止と新たな炉の設置が必要となります。イギリスでは現在7ヶ所15基の原子炉が稼働していますが、そのほとんどで老朽化が進んでいます。しかし、風力などの再生可能エネルギーの普及に伴い、安全性やコストを理由に脱原発の声が高まっており、新たな建設計画は難航しています。ヒンクリー・ポイントB原子力発電所では2つの原子炉が稼働中ですが、いずれも2022年に停止予定となっており、2016年より新たにC原発の建設が開始されたものの、なおも反対運動が行われています。今回のニュースにあるように、サイズウェル原子力発電所では、稼働中のB原発に加えてC原発の建設計画が進められていますが、反対の署名運動が行われており、すでに2万人近くが賛同しています。

　2020年11月、ボリス・ジョンソン首相は気候変動への対策と雇用の機会創出を実現すべく「グリーン産業革命のための10項目（The Ten Point Plan for a Green Industrial Revolution）」を発表し、約120億ポンド（約1兆6,000億円）の資金投入と25万人の雇用支援を打ち出しました。これらの10項目の中には、洋上風力、水素、そして原子力をクリーンエネルギーとして重視し拡大する計画が盛り込まれており、原子力の推進には、大規模発電所の建設や最新の炉の開発などが含まれています。政府が低炭素によるエネルギーミックスの実現を目指す中、原発の建設計画が今後どのような動きを見せるのかが注目されます。

参考：
https://www.nationalgrideso.com/news/record-breaking-2020-becomes-greenest-year-britains-electricity
https://www.gov.uk/government/publications/the-ten-point-plan-for-a-green-industrial-revolution

5 Filling Gaps | News Story |

CD2-11 [Original] CD2-12 [Voiced]

▶ **Watch the news, then fill the gaps in the text.**

Newsreader: The BBC has learned that the government is close to giving the green light to a new nuclear power station at Sizewell in Suffolk. Nuclear currently generates around 20% of the UK's electricity supply, although all but one of the UK's plants is due to be (¹   ) by 2030. Six sites for new plants had been (²   ), but of those, three projects have collapsed, and only one, at Hinkley in Somerset is currently under construction. The government will outline plans next month, for the UK to get to net zero carbon emissions by 2050, and have told the BBC they remain committed to new nuclear in order to hit that target. Our business editor Simon Jack looks now at the reasons why Sizewell is expected to get the go-ahead.

Simon Jack: This is what new nuclear power looks like. Construction on an (³   ) scale. Hinkley Point in Somerset is in year four of a nine-year build. It was meant to be the first of a new fleet of reactors, (⁴   ) a new nuclear age. The plan has always been to make a low-carbon copy of it right here, Sizewell in Suffolk. Three other nuclear projects have collapsed. So, if the government's still (⁵   ) to new nuclear, which it insists it is, this is really the only game in town. Making another will be cheaper, faster, while supporting and creating thousands of high-skilled jobs, according to the people who want to build it.

Jack: Sizewell B, just there. And, and presumably this is where Sizewell C will sit.

Julia Pyke, EDF Energy: Yeah, that's right.

Pyke: So, nuclear design takes a long time to get approved for each individual country, but we've, the great news is that we've got a design approved for Hinkley, and we're building it. And at Hinkley you can see (⁶   ), the copy effect in action. And that's what we want to bring to Sizewell. We want to bring the known design and that great experience, so that Sizewell starts where Unit Two of Hinkley stops, more (⁷   ), great UK content, and really building skills.

Jack: This spot right here is where Reactor Number Two of Sizewell C will go. It will take around 10 years to build and cost the best part of 20 billion pounds. There are cheaper ways of making electricity, and arguably there are greener ways, but in the future we're going to need (⁸   ) amounts of low-carbon electricity. And once they're up and running, that's what nuclear gives you.

Jack: Just a few miles up the coast, you can find one big reason why nuclear is (⁹   ). If you head out to sea, 30 miles off-shore from Lowestoft, wind farms like this have been a game-changer. The price of electricity produced by these turbines has fallen by over 70%, in the last 10 years.

Jack: A single blade on there is bigger than a football pitch and the tips might not look like it but are moving at more than 200 miles an hour. A single (**10**   )   40 can power a home for two days. And as these turbines have become bigger, so they've become more (**11**   ) and the cost has come down, making this one of the greenest and cheapest ways of making electricity.

Jack: The government wants to see tens of thousands of new and bigger turbines around the coast of the UK, enough to power every home. It can be done, says the operator 45 here, but it's a (**12**   ) target.

Keith Anderson, Chief Executive, Scottish Power ： There has to be a (**13**   ) investment into the grid, to get it ready. What you can't do, and we can't afford to do as a country, is build the wind farms, electrify all the cars, and electrify all the (**14**   ), and then find you can't plug it into the system. 50

Jack: Wind power is cheaper than nuclear, but the wind doesn't always blow, which is why (**15**   ) comparisons with nuclear are unhelpful, according to energy experts.

Professor Dieter Helm, Oxford University: Simply an either-or discussion is quite, um, a (**16**   ) way of trying to work out how to get over the next 30 55 years from here to there. Nobody thinks that nuclear is going to solve all the problems, but then it's quite hard to work out how (**17**   ) wind could solve all the problems, and indeed neither of them claim that to be the case.

Jack: Unions say there is (**18**   ) industrial logic to transfer jobs, skills and new opportunities from Somerset to Suffolk. Local reaction is divided between jobs 60 and (**19**   ), but the government insists new nuclear will be part of a low-carbon mix, which is why Sizewell C looks increasingly likely to get a green light, to be part of a green energy future. Simon Jack, BBC News.

(Friday 30 October 2020)

Notes

l.4 **Sizewell**「サイズウェル」サフォーク州の沿岸にある地域。サイズウェル原子力発電所がある　l.4 **Suffolk**「サフォーク」イングランド南西部の州　l.9 **Hinkley**「ヒンクリー」サマセット州のブリストル海峡沿いにあるヒンクリー・ポイントC原子力発電所（Hinkley Point C nuclear power station）を指す l.9 **Somerset**「サマセット」イングランド東部の州　l.15 **Hinkley Point**「ヒンクリー・ポイント」ヒンクリー・ポイントC原子力発電所のこと　l.23 **EDF Energy**「EDFエナジー」ロンドンにあるフランス電力（EDF: Électricité de France）傘下の総合エネルギー企業。2002年設立　l.36 **Lowestoft**「ローストフト」サフォーク州にある北海沿岸の港町　l.47 **Scottish Power**「スコティッシュ・パワー」1990年にグラスゴーで設立された電力会社　l.61 **a low-carbon mix**「低炭素（エネルギー）ミックス」エネルギーミックス（energy mix）とは、エネルギーの安定供給、経済性、環境保全を実現するために、多様なエネルギー資源をバランス良く組み合わせた電源構成のことを言う

放射能の発見

　放射能の第１発見者はフランスの物理学者アンリ・ベクレル（Henri Becquerel, 1852-1908）で、1896年にウランの硫酸塩から放射能が出ていることを発見しました。その発見に目をつけ、翌年より研究を引き継いだのがマリー・キュリー（Marie Curie, 1867-1934）で、夫ピエール・キュリー（Pierre Curie, 1859-1906）と共にラジウム、およびポロニウムを発見しました。ベクレルは1903年、キュリー夫妻は1905年に、ノーベル物理学賞を受賞しました。マリーは夫の死後、ラジウムの分離に成功し、1911年には２度目のノーベル賞を今度は化学の分野で受賞しました。ノーベル賞授章式でピエール・キュリーは、「ラジウムが悪の手に渡れば、世の中に危害をもたらすでしょう。危険かもしれないこの知識を、われわれはきちんと受け止めることができるだろうか」と警告を発しています。イギリスでのキュリー夫妻の評価は高く、2018年には歴史専門誌『BBCヒストリー』（*BBC History*）による「世界を変えた女性100人」の第１位にマリーが選ばれました。

Moving On　　6 Making a Summary　 CD2-13

▶ **Fill the gaps to complete the summary.**

　　About 20% of the UK's electricity is generated by nuclear power, but all except one of the plants will be (d　　　　　　　　) by 2030. At present only one plant is being built, at Hinkley, Somerset, but it is expected that the government will give the (g　　　　　) for a new plant at Sizewell, in Suffolk. It will be a (r　　　　　　) of the Hinkley plant, and therefore should be easier to build. It will take about 10 years to build and cost nearly 20 billion pounds. However, the construction is (c　　　　　　), because the price of electricity generated by wind turbines has fallen by 70% in 10 years. The government wants enough wind turbines to power every home, but the operator says this is a (f　　　　　　) target. It would require (c　　　　　　) investments into the grid, so that wind power can be plugged into the system. It might be cheaper than nuclear, but because the wind doesn't always blow, (b　　　　　) comparisons are unhelpful. A simple 'either nuclear or wind' discussion is a (c　　　　　　) way to decide policy. Some local people in Sizewell are concerned about (d　　　　　　), but unions say there is (c　　　　　) logic to transfer jobs and opportunities from Somerset to Suffolk.

7 Follow Up

▶ **Discuss, write or present.**

1. What do you know about nuclear power in Japan? How many nuclear plants are there?

2. What are the arguments against nuclear power?

3. What do you think? Should we continue to develop nuclear power, or should we halt it?

Unit 13

Meat Grown in the Laboratory

代替肉への関心が世界で高まる中、シンガポールでは世界で初めてある食肉の販売が認可されました。一体どのような食品なのでしょうか。ニュースを見てみましょう。

Starting Off

1 Setting the Scene

▶ **What do you think?**

1. Are you concerned about eating healthily? Do you have a healthy diet?
2. Do you like meat? How much meat do you eat?
3. Have you ever thought about not eating meat? Do you know anybody who doesn't eat meat? Are they healthy?

2 Building Language

▶ **For each word (1-6), find two synonyms (a-l).**

1. cultured   [   ][   ]
2. slaughterhouse [   ][   ]
3. nutrient   [   ][   ]
4. embrace   [   ][   ]
5. disrupt   [   ][   ]
6. unintended   [   ][   ]

a. grown
b. interrupt
c. acceptance
d. food
e. cultivated
f. break

g. butchery
h. nourishment
i. accidental
j. abattoir
k. adoption
l. inadvertent

3 Understanding Check 1

▶ Read the quotes, then watch the news and match them to the right people.

1. Some people are always going to come to butcher shops like this one ...
   [   ]

2. It is an open door to sell meat ...
   [   ]

3. ... I'm a foodie at heart, so to me flavour always has to come first.
   [   ]

4. ... so increasing local production capability is the key ...   [   ]

4 Understanding Check 2

▶ Which is the best answer?

1. The co-founder of Eat Just mentioned three advantages of cultured meat. Which of the following did he <u>not</u> mention?
   a. They don't have to worry about food safety.
   b. They don't have to keep it in a refrigerator.
   c. They don't have to cut down any trees.
   d. They don't have to kill any animals.

2. Why is Singapore embracing meat alternatives?
   a. Meat alternatives will soon be very cheap.
   b. Real meat is very unhealthy.
   c. They are concerned that they might not be able to import enough food.
   d. The people of Singapore don't want to kill animals for food.

3. What food are they planning to sell next?
   a. lab-grown fish
   b. lab-grown turkey
   c. lab-grown beef
   d. lab-grown pork

▶ **What do you remember?**

4. What is cultured meat grown from?

_____

5. According to Barclays, how much will the cultured meat market be worth?

_____

6. What did the three people at the end think about lab-grown meat?

_____

BACKGROUND INFORMATION

　代替肉とは、本物の動物の肉ではなく、大豆などの植物を原料として肉の風味や食感を再現した食品のことです。昨今では、ヴィーガンやベジタリアンなど、菜食に関心を持つ人々が世界中で増加しており、①動物を殺して食べることへの倫理的な反発、②畜産によって生じる温室効果ガスなどの環境負荷への懸念、③人口増加に伴う食料不足への危惧などの理由で代替肉の需要も拡大しつつあります。イギリスでは、2006年には15万人だったヴィーガンの数が、2018年には60万人に増加しました。また、肉を使わない食品の売り上げも、2015年の約5億3,900万ポンド（約754億円）から、2018年には約7億4,000万ポンド（約1,360億円）に増加しました。2020年には、大手スーパーマーケットのテスコ（Tesco）が、代替肉等の植物由来食品の売り上げを2025年までに300％増加する目標を発表しており、市場のさらなる拡大が期待されています。

　今回のニュースの舞台であるシンガポールでは、2020年、世界に先駆けて動物の細胞から人工的に作り出した培養肉の国内における販売が認められました。その背景には、政府が2019年から取り組んでいる「30バイ30（30 by 30）」という目標があります。現在、シンガポールは食料の約90％を輸入に頼っており、食料自給率は10％以下となっていますが、これを2030年までに30％に引き上げるべく、約1億4,400万シンガポールドル（約119億5,000万円、1シンガポールドル＝約82円）の研究資金を投じて、食品や農業における技術開発に力を注いでいます。その最中、2020年に新型コロナウイルスのパンデミックが発生したことで、従来の食肉の生産や流通システムの脆弱性が露呈し、食料安全保障の必要性がいっそう高まりました。そのため、フードテック分野への投資による、より安定した食料供給の実現が早急な課題となっています。様々な企業が続々と参入を始めており、シンガポールは代替肉・培養肉の一大拠点となりつつあります。しかし、通常の肉よりも値段が割高であることから、培養肉の一般家庭への普及はまだ先のことになりそうです。また、人体への影響や安全面を懸念する声もあります。生産過程で排出される二酸化炭素や資源の消費量などについても未知な部分が多く、今後の長期的な研究結果が待たれています。

参考：
https://www.bbc.com/news/business-44488051
https://www.sfa.gov.sg/food-farming/singapore-food-story/r-and-d-programme
https://www.straitstimes.com/singapore/strengthening-food-security-with-rd

5 Filling Gaps

News Story

▶ Watch the news, then fill the gaps in the text.

Sarah Toms: This chicken never had (¹   ) or a beak. In the future of food, the lab is replacing the (²   ), by creating meat from animal stem cells.

First man: I'm going to make the best chicken nuggets ever.

Toms: In a world first, the California startup, Eat Just, has (³   ) to sell (⁴   ) chicken, that will soon come to a restaurant in Singapore.

Josh Tetrick, co-founder of Eat Just: It is an open door to sell meat without killing an animal, without (⁵   ) a rainforest, without all the land and carbon and food safety risks.

Toms: The cells are fed with (⁶   ) and kept warm in a special (⁷   ). In four to six weeks, they become meat.

Toms: William Chen, an advisor to the government, says Singapore's (⁸   ) of meat alternatives reflects its concerns about food security, as a small country that (⁹   ) on imports for almost everything.

Professor William Chen, Nanyang Technological University: This import of food chain can be (¹⁰   ), so increasing local production capability is the key and the, the, the idea here is to (¹¹   ) consumers with a local produced food, as a option.

Toms: Eat Just is not the only company bringing science to the table. Shiok Meats is a Singapore startup looking to (¹²   ) diners with its lab-grown shrimp, and at 300 dollars for one shrimp dumpling, the price tag is out of reach for many.

Toms: Some people are always going to come to butcher shops like this one to get their meat. But the appetite for meat (¹³   ) is growing due to concerns about health, animal welfare, and the environment. Barclays estimates the (¹⁴   ) meat market could be worth 140 billion US dollars by the end of this (¹⁵   ). Well, what do people here in Singapore think about eating chicken grown in a lab?

Second man: If the (¹⁶   ) is there, there's always a possibility to carry these products and, er, I don't see why not.

Woman: I, I'm a little bit concerned about, er, you know, the (**17**   ), er, side effects.

Third man: I mean, I'll (**18**   ) try it, but, er, I'm a foodie at heart, so to me flavour always has to come first.

Toms: In Singapore, chicken is just the start. (**19**   ) burgers may now be next. Eat Just plans to (**20**   ) next year to sell lab-grown beef. The future of food is almost here. Sarah Toms, BBC News, Singapore.

(Thursday 10 December 2020)

Notes

l.8 **Eat Just**「イート・ジャスト」アメリカのサンフランシスコに本社を置く食品会社。2011年設立 l.16 **food security**「食料安全保障」食料の供給、アクセス、安定性を国家レベルで確保すること。国際連合食料農業機関（FAO: Food and Agriculture Organization of the United Nations）の定義によれば、「全ての人々がいかなる時も活動的で健康的な生活に必要な食のニーズと嗜好を満たすために、十分で安全かつ栄養のある食料を、物理的、経済的にも入手可能である時、食料安全保障が実現している」 l.18 **Nanyang Technological University**「ナンヤン工科大学」1991年に設立されたシンガポールの国立大学。中国語名は南洋理工大学 l.21 **as a option** 文法的に正しくは as an option となる l.22 **Shiok Meats**「シオック・ミーツ」2018年に設立された、エビ、カニ、ロブスターなどの甲殻類の培養肉を開発するシンガポールの会社。2022年の製品化を目指している l.27 **animal welfare**「動物福祉」感受性を持つ生き物として動物に接し、人間が動物に与える痛みやストレスを最小限に抑えようとする考え方 l.27 **Barclays**「バークレイズ」ロンドンに本部がある国際金融グループ。1896年設立

急成長するフェイクミート市場

　イギリスでは、ヴィーガンのファストフードの人気が急上昇しています。また出前のチェーンでもヴィーガンやフェイクミートのメニューが人気新商品の上位に入るなど、確実に市場が拡大しています。アメリカでは2009年創業の「ビヨンド・ミート（Beyond Meat）」がケンタッキー・フライド・チキンと、また「インポッシブル・フーズ（Impossible Foods）」がバーガーキングと業務提携し、その商品が爆発的な人気を誇っています。長年、大衆層の食と健康が社会的課題となっていたアメリカでは、SNS等の影響もあり、近年健康志向がブームとなりました。環境問題への意識の高まりもあり、菜食が広まっています。そのような中、投資という要因が加わって、フェイクミート企業が躍進しています。2021年1月には、創業から半年余りの日本の代替肉スタートアップの「ネクストミーツ」が、「特別買収目的会社（SPAC: Special Purpose Acquisition Company）」という仕組みを使い、アメリカの準備市場に上場しました。和食という「文化遺産」を武器に、アメリカ市場に切り込む構えです。

Moving On　　　**6** Making a Summary　　　 CD2-16

▶ **Fill the gaps to complete the summary.**

　The lab is beginning to replace the (s_____). Barclays estimates the (c_____) meat market could be worth 140 billion US dollars by 2030, as the appetite for meat substitutes grows due to concerns about health, animal welfare, and the environment. Singapore is concerned that food imports might be (d_____), so it has (e_____) meat alternatives. One company, Eat Just, from California, has received (a_____) to sell (c_____) chicken, and are applying to sell cultured beef next year. They say that it is an opportunity to sell meat without killing an animal or deforesting a rainforest. They feed (n_____) to stem cells, which then grow into meat in four to six weeks. Another company, Shiok Meats, from Singapore, is selling expensive lab-grown shrimps. However, one woman interviewed said she was concerned about (u_____) side effects.

7 Follow Up

▶ **Discuss, write or present.**

1. What do you think about lab-grown meat? Have you ever eaten it? Would you eat it if someone offered it to you?

2. The reporter said "The future of food is almost here." Do you agree with her? Do you think that in ten years, most of our meat will be lab-grown?

3. In what ways has the food we eat changed in the last thirty years?

Unit 14

Cardiff, the First Carbon Neutral City in Wales

加速化する気候変動への対応が迫られる中、ウェールズの首都カーディフは、カーボン・ニュートラルを実現する宣言をしました。果たして可能なのでしょうか。ニュースを見てみましょう。

Starting Off

1 Setting the Scene

▶ What do you think?

1. Have you, or your family, ever grown vegetables to eat? Do you think it is easy to do?
2. In the town or city where you live, do you often see places where food is grown?
3. In what ways do you think that growing food in the city might be good for the environment?

2 Building Language

▶ Which word (1-5) best fits which explanation (a-e)?

1. slash   [   ]   **a.** reduce severely and suddenly
2. embedded   [   ]   **b.** a device for burning something, usually garbage, until it is ashes
3. landfill   [   ]   **c.** disposal of waste by burying it in the earth
4. incinerator   [   ]   **d.** set up, organise, and begin
5. launch   [   ]   **e.** fixed into, or part of something

Watching the News

3 Understanding Check 1

▶ Read the quotes, then watch the news and match them to the right people.

1. So we are looking at anything we can. [   ]
2. You know, that's why we need to change, as a council, as a city. [   ]
3. All of Wales's councils are working towards a Welsh government target ... [   ]
4. It includes more green energy schemes, tree planting, and city farms. [   ]

4 Understanding Check 2

▶ Which is the best answer?

1. The woman in the Cardiff Salad Garden gave three reasons why it is important for food to be local. Which of the following did she not mention?
   a. The food will be fresh because it is delivered quickly.
   b. The food will be cheaper because transport costs are low.
   c. Food contains a lot of embedded energy, which shouldn't be wasted.
   d. It's completely sustainable because the farm is inside the city.

2. Which of the following sentences is correct, according to the video?
   a. Cardiff has cut carbon emissions by about 49% in five or six years.
   b. Cardiff will build better LED lampposts.
   c. Cardiff is planning to build 20 Principality Stadiums.
   d. Cardiff is planning to cut carbon emissions by 49% within five or six years.

3. What is the difference between the Welsh government's climate target, and Cardiff's climate target?
   a. By 2030, the Welsh government aims to be completely carbon neutral, but in Cardiff only the public sector will be carbon neutral.
   b. There is no difference. They are both aiming to be carbon neutral as soon as possible.
   c. The Welsh government's target is much more ambitious than Cardiff's target.
   d. Cardiff aims to be completely carbon neutral by 2030, but the Welsh government isn't aiming to be completely neutral until 2050.

4. What does Cardiff's new plan to slash carbon emissions include?

_____

5. What did Cardiff Council and the Welsh Government spend 10 million pounds on?

_____

6. Why have the council launched a consultation?

_____

BACKGROUND INFORMATION

　2019年、イギリス政府は二酸化炭素排出量と吸収量を差し引きゼロにするというカーボン・ニュートラル（carbon neutral）の目標を2050年に設定しました。それに先立ち、ウェールズ政府は2016年に制定した「ウェールズ環境法（Environment (Wales) Act 2016）」において二酸化炭素排出の削減を義務付け、ウェールズ全体でのカーボン・ニュートラル実現の目標を2050年に設定しました。また、2017年には各自治体の公共機関で2030年までにカーボン・ニュートラルを実現するという目標を立てました。結果として、ウェールズ全体では2018年までに1990年代と比較して31%の温室効果ガスを削減しました。今後は2030年までに63%、2040年までに89%、2050年までに100%を実現する計画です。

　しかし、ウェールズの首都であるカーディフの状況は他の都市に比べて切実なものとなっています。アメリカの気候研究機関クライメート・セントラル（Climate Central）は、もし気温が今の状況で上がり続け、二酸化炭素排出量の大幅な削減もなく対策も施されなければ、カーディフを含む南ウェールズは2050年までに水没し、平均300万人の人々が年に1回は洪水の被害を受けると発表しました。このような危機的状況にあるカーディフは2019年3月28日、気候非常事態（Climate Emergency）を宣言しました。その気候非常事態宣言に対する具体的な返答として、2020年10月15日、「ワン・プラネット・カーディフ（One Planet Cardiff）」という政策が議会で承認され、イギリスやウェールズ全体よりも20年早く、2030年までに市全体でカーボン・ニュートラルを実現させるという目標を立てました。具体的には、①エネルギー効率の良い建物の建設や補修、②水力・風力発電、LEDの街灯、暖房システムの開発を通じたエネルギー削減、③公共交通の見直しと歩行者・自転車用道路の改善、④市内の植樹面積の19%から25%への増加、⑤地元における食材の生産、⑥リサイクルの増加とゴミの削減、⑦排水の整備などによる洪水防止といった7つの観点から、カーボン・ニュートラルを積極的に推し進める計画です。すでにカーディフでは2005年以降、公共機関の二酸化炭素排出量が45%、家庭からの排出量は38%、産業・商業セクターにおいては55%削減されています。イギリスだけでなく世界中の他の都市に先駆けてカーボン・ニュートラルへの道を突き進むカーディフの今後が注目されています。

参考：

https://www.oneplanetcardiff.co.uk/
https://www.walesonline.co.uk/news/wales-news/sea-level-climate-change-wales-18695700

Unit 14　Cardiff, the First Carbon Neutral City in Wales　　81

5 Filling Gaps | News Story

▶ **Watch the news, then fill the gaps in the text.**

Newsreader: Wales's capital can set an example by becoming a carbon neutral city within a decade. That's the ambitious claim from the leader of Cardiff council, Huw Thomas, as a new plan to (¹   )   5 (²   ) is set to be approved by his cabinet this week. It includes more green energy schemes, tree planting, and city farms. Our environmental correspondent, Steffan Messenger, reports.

Steffan Messenger: Growing crops in the heart of the capital. The Cardiff Salad Garden (³   ) local restaurants and delivers direct to people's homes 10 by bike, from their base in this city centre park.

Sophie Bolton, Cardiff Salad Garden: Local food is really important. There's a lot of (⁴   ) energy in the food that we eat. This salad gets picked and delivered to people within two hours, so you're having a completely fresh food (⁵   ). And, also, it's coming from right in the city. That's completely 15 (⁶   ).

Messenger: To cut back on the environmental impact associated with transporting food into the city, the local council wants to see more ventures like this one take off. There are plans for a hydroponics unit nearby which could fit three acres (⁷   ) of crops into one shipping container. A large city farm, and veg 20 planting plots on new housing developments are also proposed. It's all part of a strategy to try and cut the capital's (⁸   ) emissions dramatically by the end of the decade.

Messenger: All of Wales's councils are working towards a Welsh government target for a carbon neutral public sector by 2030, so, (⁹   ) emissions in the areas 25 they have influence over. But Cardiff says it wants to go further, and end the entire city's (¹⁰   ) to global warming by the same year.

Messenger: It's a huge challenge, given that Wales and the UK aren't set to meet a similar goal before 2050. The council hopes projects like this new solar park — it's built 30 on an old (¹¹   ) site, the size of 20 Principality Stadiums — will help.

Councillor Michael Michael, Cabinet Member for the Environment: We've already, er, while we've been working on this, er, cut our (¹²   ) down by something like 49% over the last five, six years. Solar power is just one of them, LED (¹³   ) another one. Er, Building Better. So we are looking at anything we can.

Messenger: Other schemes include underground pipes to carry heat from this waste (¹⁴   ) to warm buildings, so they don't need gas, reopening old canals to manage water more (¹⁵   ) and prevent flooding, and covering 25% of the city in trees to (¹⁶   ) up emissions. The council's leader says urgent action's needed, given the threat posed to Cardiff as a coastal capital.

Councillor Huw Thomas, Leader, Cardiff Council: Well, we're obviously anxious. That's why we, alongside the Welsh government, are spending over 10 million pounds, again, just behind me on, er, a flood defence (¹⁷   ) for this part of the city. Um, but that alone won't be enough. You know, that's why we need to change, as a council, as a city. And why we need to set an example for others to follow as well.

Messenger: While the council's cabinet is set to approve the new strategy this week, questions remain about whether the time (¹⁸   ) involved are (¹⁹   ). A consultation's been (²⁰   ) to seek ideas from the public, and try to get them on board.

(Tuesday 13 October 2020)

Notes

l.4 **Cardiff**「カーディフ」ウェールズ南部の市・海港で、ウェールズの首都　l.9 **The Cardiff Salad Garden**「カーディフ・サラダ・ガーデン」2017年に活動を開始した非営利社会事業　l.32 **Principality Stadium**「プリンシパリティ・スタジアム」カーディフにあるスタジアムで、ラグビーやサッカーに使われる。開閉式屋根を持ち、全天候対応型となっている。別名「ナショナルスタジアム・オブ・ウェールズ (National Stadium of Wales)」とも「ミレニアム・スタジアム (Millennium Stadium)」とも呼ぶ。敷地面積4万平方メートル。1999年開場　l.40 **Building Better**「ビルディング・ベター」イギリスの住宅産業におけるスローガンで、建設の効率化、品質の向上、二酸化炭素の削減などを掲げている

BEHIND THE SCENES

城の街、カーディフ

　ウェールズで最も環境に優しい都市として発展しつつあるカーディフですが、実は、1平方マイルあたりの城の数で世界一を誇っています。「カーディフ」とは「タフ川の要塞 (the fort of the Taff)」という意味で、1世紀にローマ人によって築かれた砦を起源としています。市内にはおよそ20の城や城塞跡があります。最も有名なのは街の中心部にあるカーディフ城 (Cardiff Castle) で、ローマ人の城塞を基として11世紀にノルマン人によって建設されました。その後、19世紀のヴィクトリア朝時代に改装が行われ、現在のゴシック・リヴァイヴァル建築の特徴を兼ね備えた建築物になりました。また、街の北部に位置し、ウェールズ語で「赤い城」を意味するコッホ城 (Castell Coch) も、11世紀のノルマン人の城塞を19世紀に改装したものです。新旧の歴史を保ちながら発展してきたカーディフの今後が注目されます。

Moving On　　　**6** Making a Summary CD2-19

▶ **Fill the gaps to complete the summary.**

　　Wales and the rest of the UK aim to be carbon neutral by 2050, while the Welsh public sector will be carbon neutral by 2030. However, Cardiff is planning to (s　　　　　　) carbon (e　　　　　　), and be totally carbon neutral by 2030. It will build a new solar park on an old (l　　　　　　) site, and pipes to carry heat from a waste (i　　　　　　) to warm buildings. It will also reopen canals, and encourage farms to grow crops in the heart of the capital and cover 25% of the city in trees, which soak up (e　　　　　　).　One such farm, the Cardiff Salad Garden, supplies restaurants and delivers direct to homes by bike. The manager believes that it is important for food production to be local, as there is a lot of (e　　　　　　) energy in the food we eat. If it is delivered quickly, it is fresh. It is also (s　　　　　　) because it comes locally, from the city.　Finally, because Cardiff is a coastal capital, they are spending 10 million pounds on a flood defense scheme. However, it is not certain that these targets are (a　　　　　　), and a consultation has been (l　　　　　　) to seek ideas from the public.

7 Follow Up

▶ **Discuss, write or present.**

1. Do a little research and find out if the town or city where you live has a similar policy to reduce carbon emissions.
2. If local food is delivered to you from the farm by bike, would you buy it instead of going to the supermarket?
3. Cardiff plans to cover 25% of the city in trees to soak up emissions. What do you think of that idea?

Unit 15

Brexit Problems at the Border

イギリスの EU 離脱が、ヨーロッパとの貿易に波紋を広げています。一体どのような問題が生じているのでしょうか。ニュースを見てみましょう。

Starting Off

1 Setting the Scene

▶ **What do you think?**

1. What is Brexit? How do you think it will change the trade between Europe and the United Kingdom?
2. Do you know what things Japan exports to the United Kingdom?
3. If you are exporting meat to another country, what would be the most important things to consider?

2 Building Language

▶ **Which word (1-6) best fits which explanation (a-f)?**

1. perishable   [   ]   **a.** so crowded that it is difficult to move
2. abattoir   [   ]   **b.** time that something can stay in the shop before it goes bad or unusable
3. shelf-life   [   ]   **c.** a person or company that transports goods by lorry
4. haulier   [   ]   **d.** liable to rot or go bad
5. congested   [   ]   **e.** the place where animals are killed for food; slaughterhouse
6. friction-free   [   ]   **f.** smooth; without delay or complication

3 Understanding Check 1

▶ Read the quotes, then watch the news and match them to the right people.

1. ... additional complexity on trading with our biggest trading partner, are here to stay.   [   ]

2. Exports are grinding to a halt at the moment.   [   ]

3. ... last week for me was the, probably the worst, most difficult week I've had in this job ...   [   ]

4. For fresh quality product, trading on a daily basis, this system is not fit for purpose, and it needs to be looked at urgently.   [   ]

4 Understanding Check 2

▶ Which is the best answer?

1. Which one of the following sentences is correct?
    a. The UK exports 15 billion pounds worth of perishable meat, fish, and fish produce to the EU every year.
    b. The UK exports 25% of its meat and fish to the EU every year.
    c. Currently, the UK is only exporting a quarter of the volume of meat that they usually do at this time of year.
    d. A third of the meat which the UK exports to the EU is perishable.

2. Which of the following trading problems was not mentioned?
    a. Paperwork takes much longer than before.
    b. Car parks are full and the roads are congested.
    c. Exporters have to pay a lot more money to the hauliers.
    d. Shelf-life is being shortened because of all the delays in transport.

3. What does the reporter say about the future?
    a. Trade with the EU will probably continue to be more expensive and complicated.
    b. These problems will be short-lived because volumes are expected to increase.
    c. When ports start to operate again at normal volumes, the problems will be less serious.
    d. If ports carry on operating at less than their normal volumes, there will certainly be chaos.

▶ **What do you remember?**

4. Customers are frustrated and considering other options. What does one customer say that he might do?

_____

5. According to Stephen Cock, there will be problems not only with exports, but also with imports. Why?

_____

6. What does the government say that it is doing about the problems?

_____

BACKGROUND INFORMATION

　イギリスは、2016年6月23日に行われた国民投票でEU離脱を決定し、2020年1月31日に正式に離脱しました。2020年のほぼ1年間は移行期間とされ、2020年12月31日午後11時にその期間が終了すると、EU法は適用されなくなりました。離脱が完了して迎えた2021年1月、イギリスからEUへの肉の輸出量は空前の最低値を記録しました。その背景には新型コロナウイルス感染症によるロックダウンの影響で外食産業が不振に陥ったという事情もありますが、ニュースにあるように煩雑な輸出手続きが大きな障害になっているということもあります。

　2020年まで、EU各国内に肉を輸出するのは、イギリス国内の輸送とほとんど変わりませんでした。精肉業者は、出荷通知書と商品配達受領書を製品と共に運転手に渡し、運転手はフランスのカレーに渡り、そのまま卸業者に届けることができました。しかし、正式離脱以降、この同じ輸出に26段階の手続きが必要になりました。EUとの輸出入の手続きとして、精肉業者、運転手、そして卸売業者が度々オンライン上のシステムにアクセスする必要があり、また、精肉業者は環境食料農林省（DEFRA: Department for Environment, Food and Rural Affairs）に認可された検査官である獣医などの訪問を受け、製品検査後、衛生証明書を発行してもらわなければなりません。しかし、認可検査官の数が少なく、各種手続きに膨大な時間が費やされており、2021年1月の精肉のEUへの輸出額は、2020年の同月に比べて52％減少しました。

　新たな体制の開始に伴う混乱は否めませんが、システムの構造そのものの改善を求める声も多く聞かれます。1つの可能性として、スイスの前例に倣い、EUと審査基準を統一して共通の製品審査制度を設ける、というものがあります。また、デンマーク、オランダ、ドイツのように、認可検査官の最終承認以前の段階を担う検査官を育成する制度も提案されています。EU以外への輸出の伸びで（食肉産業の）危機は回避されたものの、隣国との円滑な貿易のため、EU離脱後のイギリスには解決すべき問題が山積しています。

参考：
https://www.fwi.co.uk/business/markets-and-trends/meat-prices/post-brexit-eu-meat-exports-down-52-year-on-year
https://ukandeu.ac.uk/the-british-meat-export-system-post-brexit/

5 Filling Gaps | News Story |

▶ **Watch the news, then fill the gaps in the text.**

Newsreader: British meat exporters say new customs systems post-Brexit are not fit for purpose. (^{1}) goods are being delayed for hours, sometimes days, because of (^{2}) customs checks and additional paperwork. The new border rules were (^{3}) two weeks ago at the end of the Brexit transition period. The UK exports 15 billion pounds worth of food and drink to the EU every year. A third of it is (^{4}) meat, fish, and fresh produce. The trade body says meat exports to the EU are (^{5}) at 25% of their normal volumes for this time of year. Our business editor Simon Jack's report begins at a meat processing factory in Shropshire.

Simon Jack: UK lamb is highly prized. At this Shropshire-based (^{6}), 70% gets exported to the EU. It's an export-driven success story. But the well-oiled machine that gets it there has a new spanner in it. Paperwork that used to take 15 minutes is now taking hours, and also (^{7}) vet certificates not needed before.

Rizvan Khalid, Managing Director, Euro Quality Lambs: So, we've been having sleepless nights. We've been taking calls from the (^{8}), from the agents, early hours of the morning. It has been a (^{9}), steep learning curve, and we see some of these problems will (^{10}), even once we get to the new normal level. For fresh quality product, trading on a daily basis, this system is not fit for purpose, and it needs to be looked at urgently.

Jack: Rizvan's products are still getting through, but delays are shortening (^{11}), making his customers frustrated and forcing them to (^{12}) other options.

Francis Ocha, Fory Viandes: I feel very upset about, about this situation. So, we are thinking to buy some lambs in the, in Spain. So, we have some er, er, of our competitors who are, order their lambs ... in Ireland instead of, er, instead of UK.

Jack: Between the seller and the buyer are the (^{13}). No one is feeling more frustrated than Pete White.

Pete White, Transport Manager, Whites Transport Services: We travel all over Western Europe, every (^{14}) week. Um, and, the, last week for me was the, probably the worst, most difficult week I've had in this job in, in twenty years. We have lost hundreds of hours, don-, dozens of days already with our, with our trucks that are waiting (**15**   ).

Stephen Cock, Customs Consultant: Behind us here, we're looking at the new, er, border control post the customs have set up.

Jack: Near the (**16**   ) of the Eurotunnel in Kent, customs expert Stephen Cock says problems on the way out, mean problems on the way in.

Cock: We have a situation where Border Force's car park is (**17**   ), er, the roads are heavily (**18**   ), they're turning lorries back now. Exports are grinding to a halt at the moment. If you've got a lorry that is going to get stuck on its way out, then if you're the (**19**   ), why would you want to bring it in in the first place? So, it will snarl everything up, import and export.

Jack: It has been a pretty miserable time for (**20**   ), for their drivers, and for their commercial customers. And remember, the problems we've seen are at a time when the ports operating at a fraction of their normal volumes. Those volumes are expected to (**21**   ). And while it's hoped that any potential (**22**   ) will be short-lived, it seems clear that additional cost, additional complexity on trading with our biggest trading partner, are here to stay.

Jack: After decades of (**23**   ) trade, there was bound to be (**24**   ). The government says it's working hard with business to get to what it describes as a new normal in cross-channel trade. Simon Jack, BBC News.

(Friday 15 January 2021)

Notes

l.7 **the Brexit transition period**「EU離脱の移行期間」EU正式離脱後、イギリスにEU法が適用されなくなるまでの移行期間のこと。2020年12月31日午後11時に終了した　l.12 **Shropshire**「シュロップシャー」イングランド西部の州　l.16 **vet certificates**「衛生証明書」veterinary certificatesの略。輸出される畜産物の衛生状態を証明する書類　l.18 **Euro Quality Lambs**「ユーロ・クオリティ・ラム」シュロップシャーに拠点を置くラム肉の製造会社。1992年設立　l.20 **steep learning curve**「急勾配の学習曲線」少ない学習時間で高い習熟度を得た状態を、縦軸を習熟度、横軸を時間とするグラフで表したもの。have a steep learning curveで「短期間に多くのことを学ぶ」という意味になる。ここでは、新たに覚えなくてはならない業務が短期間で膨大な量に増えたことを表している　l.27 **Fory Viandes**「フォリー・ヴィアンド」フランスのランジス（Rungis）にある食肉の卸売業者。2009年設立　l.39 **border control post**「国境管理所」　l.42 **Eurotunnel**「ユーロトンネル」イギリスとヨーロッパ大陸とを結ぶ鉄道用の海底トンネル。英仏海峡トンネル（the Channel Tunnel）とも呼ばれる。全長約50キロ。1994年開通　l.42 **Kent**「ケント」イングランド南東部にある州　l.44 **Border Force**「国境警備隊」　l.51 **the ports**「通関地」ports of entryの略。通関手続きを行う場所のこと

BEHIND THE SCENES

車で海峡トンネルの旅

　イギリスのフォークストーン（Folkestone）とフランスのカレー（Calais）を結ぶ海峡トンネル（Channel Tunnel）は1994年に開通した総距離50.49km、海底部分の距離約37.9kmの鉄道用海底トンネルです。走行する列車としては国際高速列車のユーロスター（Eurostar）が有名ですが、車ごと電車に乗り込んで海峡を渡るユーロトンネル・ル・シャトル（Eurotunnel Le Shuttle）もあります。ル・シャトルの旅客便は全長775mあり、前方は大型バスや車高のある乗用車用の一層構造、後方は乗用車用の二層構造になっています。チケット料金は車両の大きさなどによって異なりますが、1枚につき自動車1台と乗客9名までの運賃が含まれています。車両内にはトイレ以外の設備がなく、走行中は基本的には自動車の中で過ごしますが、車を降りて貨車内で体を伸ばすこともできます。また、ル・シャトルにはトラック用の貨物便もあります。フェリーでは約100分かかるところを約35分で渡ることができ、両岸の人々にとって重要な輸送・交通手段となっています。

Moving On　　6 Making a Summary　　 CD2-22

▶ Fill the gaps to complete the summary.

　Every year, the UK exported £5 billion worth of (p   ) meat, and fresh produce to the EU. However, at the end of the Brexit (t   ) period, new customs systems were introduced, and meat exports are only at 25% of their normal volumes. From one (a   ), 70% of the lamb is usually exported, but paperwork now takes hours. These delays shorten (s   ), and so customers are considering other options, such as buying from Spain or Ireland instead. (H   ) also are feeling frustrated, as trucks are waiting for hours, and the roads are (c   ). Because trucks will get stuck leaving the country, they don't want to enter in the first place, so both imports and exports are snarled up. For decades, there has been (f   ) trade, but now there is (d   ). The government says it is working with business to get a new normal in cross-channel trade.

7 Follow Up

▶ Discuss, write or present.

1. These new border rules were introduced on the first day of 2021. Do some research to find out whether the problems have continued, or has the government really got to 'a new normal'? Some people predicted long, slow lorry queues but has that really happened?

2. What do you think the UK exports to Japan? What British-made things do you see?

3. In 2020, Britain and Japan signed a trade agreement. There is a video about it here:
   https://www.youtube.com/watch?v=XF1V5Gg_23U
   In the video it says that the UK wants to join the Trans-Pacific partnership. Why do they want to do that? Is it wise for the UK to leave the EU and enter the TPP?

このテキストのメインページ
www.kinsei-do.co.jp/plusmedia/41

次のページの QR コードを読み取る
直接ページにジャンプできます

オンライン映像配信サービス「plus⁺Media」について

本テキストの映像は plus⁺Media ページ（www.kinsei-do.co.jp/plusmedia）から、ストリーミング再生でご利用いただけます。手順は以下に従ってください。

ログインページ

ログイン

● ご利用には、ログインが必要です。
　サイトのログインページ（www.kinsei-do.co.jp/plusmedia/login）へ行き、plus⁺Media パスワード（次のページのシールをはがしたあとに印字されている数字とアルファベット）を入力します。

● パスワードは各テキストにつき 1 つです。
　有効期限は、はじめてログインした時点から 1 年間になります。

[利用方法]

次のページにある QR コード、もしくは plus⁺Media トップページ（www.kinsei-do.co.jp/plusmedia）から該当するテキストを選んで、そのテキストのメインページにジャンプしてください。

メニューページ　　　再生画面

plus+Media トップ　　　メインページ

「Video」「Audio」をタッチすると、それぞれのメニューページにジャンプしますので、そこから該当する項目を選べば、ストリーミングが開始されます。

[推奨環境]

iOS (iPhone, iPad)	OS: iOS 12 以降 ブラウザ：標準ブラウザ	Android	OS: Android 6 以降 ブラウザ：標準ブラウザ、Chrome
PC	OS: Windows 7/8/8.1/10, MacOS X　ブラウザ：Internet Explorer 10/11, Microsoft Edge, Firefox 48以降, Chrome 53以降, Safari		

※最新の推奨環境についてはウェブサイトをご確認ください。
※上記の推奨環境を満たしている場合でも、機種によってはご利用いただけない場合もあります。また、推奨環境は技術動向等により変更される場合があります。予めご了承ください。

このシールをはがすと
plus**＋**Media 利用のための
パスワードが
記載されています。

一度はがすと元に戻すことは
できませんのでご注意下さい。

◀ここからはがして下さい

4146 British News
Update 4
(BBC)

plus **＋ M** edia®

本書にはCD（別売）があります

British News Update 4

映像で学ぶ　イギリス公共放送の最新ニュース4

2022年1月20日　初版第1刷発行
2024年9月10日　初版第4刷発行

編著者　Timothy Knowles

田　中　みんね

中　村　美帆子

馬　上　紗矢香

発行者　福　岡　正　人

発行所　株式会社　金星堂

（〒101-0051）　東京都千代田区神田神保町 3-21
Tel　　（03）3263-3828（営業部）
　　　　（03）3263-3997（編集部）
Fax　　（03）3263-0716
http://www.kinsei-do.co.jp

編集担当　長島吉成　　　　　　　　　Printed in Japan
印刷所・製本所／三美印刷株式会社

ISBN978-4-7647-4146-1　C1082